# Lecture Notes in Computer Science 16146

Founding Editors

Gerhard Goos
Juris Hartmanis

Editorial Board Members

Elisa Bertino, *Purdue University, West Lafayette, IN, USA*
Wen Gao, *Peking University, Beijing, China*
Bernhard Steffen, *TU Dortmund University, Dortmund, Germany*
Moti Yung, *Columbia University, New York, NY, USA*

The series Lecture Notes in Computer Science (LNCS), including its subseries Lecture Notes in Artificial Intelligence (LNAI) and Lecture Notes in Bioinformatics (LNBI), has established itself as a medium for the publication of new developments in computer science and information technology research, teaching, and education.

LNCS enjoys close cooperation with the computer science R & D community, the series counts many renowned academics among its volume editors and paper authors, and collaborates with prestigious societies. Its mission is to serve this international community by providing an invaluable service, mainly focused on the publication of conference and workshop proceedings and postproceedings. LNCS commenced publication in 1973.

Hien Van Nguyen · Akash Awasthi ·
Vishal M. Patel · Ngan Le · Yuyin Zhou ·
Sheng Liu · S. Kevin Zhou
Editors

# Emerging LLM/LMM Applications in Medical Imaging

First International Workshop, ELAMI 2025
Held in Conjunction with MICCAI 2025
Daejeon, South Korea, September 27, 2025
Proceedings

*Editors*
Hien Van Nguyen
University of Houston
Houston, TX, USA

Akash Awasthi
University of Houston
Houston, TX, USA

Vishal M. Patel
Johns Hopkins University
Baltimore, MD, USA

Ngan Le
University of Arkansas
Fayetteville, AR, USA

Yuyin Zhou
University of California
Santa Cruz, CA, USA

Sheng Liu
Stanford University
Stanford, CA, USA

S. Kevin Zhou
Chinese Academy of Sciences
Beijing, China

ISSN 0302-9743　　　　　　　ISSN 1611-3349　(electronic)
Lecture Notes in Computer Science
ISBN 978-3-032-07501-7　　　ISBN 978-3-032-07502-4　(eBook)
https://doi.org/10.1007/978-3-032-07502-4

© The Editor(s) (if applicable) and The Author(s), under exclusive license to Springer Nature Switzerland AG 2026

This work is subject to copyright. All rights are solely and exclusively licensed by the Publisher, whether the whole or part of the material is concerned, specifically the rights of translation, reprinting, reuse of illustrations, recitation, broadcasting, reproduction on microfilms or in any other physical way, and transmission or information storage and retrieval, electronic adaptation, computer software, or by similar or dissimilar methodology now known or hereafter developed.
The use of general descriptive names, registered names, trademarks, service marks, etc. in this publication does not imply, even in the absence of a specific statement, that such names are exempt from the relevant protective laws and regulations and therefore free for general use.
The publisher, the authors and the editors are safe to assume that the advice and information in this book are believed to be true and accurate at the date of publication. Neither the publisher nor the authors or the editors give a warranty, expressed or implied, with respect to the material contained herein or for any errors or omissions that may have been made. The publisher remains neutral with regard to jurisdictional claims in published maps and institutional affiliations.

This Springer imprint is published by the registered company Springer Nature Switzerland AG
The registered company address is: Gewerbestrasse 11, 6330 Cham, Switzerland

If disposing of this product, please recycle the paper.

# Preface

This volume contains the proceedings of the Workshop on Emerging LLM/LMM Applications in Medical Imaging (ELAMI 2025), held in Daejeon, South Korea, on September 27, 2025, in conjunction with MICCAI 2025.

The workshop brought together researchers from healthcare, machine learning, and medical imaging to explore how large language models (LLMs) and large multimodal models (LMMs) are transforming the field. Topics included novel applications, interpretability, bias, and hallucination challenges, adaptive clinical workflows, and integration of LLMs into imaging pipelines.

The Program Committee received 24 submissions. Each paper underwent a rigorous double-blind peer review process with at least two expert reviewers per paper. The review criteria included:

- originality and significance
- soundness and clarity
- relevance to ELAMI topics
- quality of evaluation
- reproducibility and transparency

A total of 14 papers were accepted, resulting in an acceptance rate of 58.3%. We are deeply grateful to the reviewers for their commitment, to the authors for their contributions, and to the participants for the stimulating discussions and feedback that helped shape this emerging area of research.

We also thank the University of Houston and our sponsors for their support, and Springer for publishing this volume in the Lecture Notes in Computer Science (LNCS) series.

August 2025

Hien Van Nguyen
Akash Awasthi
Vishal M. Patel
Ngan Le
Yuyin Zhou
Sheng Liu
S. Kevin Zhou

# Organization

## General Chair

Hien Van Nguyen — University of Houston, USA

## Program Committee Chairs

Akash Awasthi — University of Houston, USA
Vishal M. Patel — Johns Hopkins University, USA
Ngan Le — University of Arkansas, USA
Yuyin Zhou — University of California, Santa Cruz, USA
Sheng Liu — Stanford University, USA
S. Kevin Zhou — Institute of Computing Technology, Chinese Academy of Sciences, China

## Reviewers

Shivanand Kundargi — University of Maryland, Baltimore County, USA
Son T. Ly — University of Houston, USA
Zihang Jiang — University of Science and Technology of China, China
Rongsheng Wang — University of Science and Technology of China, China
Qingsong Yao — Stanford University, USA
Haoran Lai — University of Science and Technology of China, China
Kun Zhang — University of Science and Technology of China, China
Aimon Rahman — Johns Hopkins University, USA
Ke Zhang — Johns Hopkins University, USA
Qingyuan Liu — Columbia University, USA
Anh M. Vu — University of Houston, USA
Haochen You — Columbia University, USA
Huy Q. Vo — University of Houston, USA
Hung Q. Vo — University of Houston, USA
Saba Khan — University of Houston, USA

| | |
|---|---|
| Qingyue Wei | Stanford University, USA |
| Juncheng Wu | University of California, Santa Cruz, USA |
| Mohammad Daouk | University of Houston, USA |
| Xiaoke Huang | University of California, Santa Cruz, USA |
| Siqi Wang | Stanford University, USA |
| Mingjie Li | Stanford University, USA |

# Contents

GMAT: Grounded Multi-agent Clinical Description Generation for Text Encoder in Vision-Language MIL for Whole Slide Image Classification ....... 1
*Ngoc Bui Lam Quang, Nam Le Nguyen Binh, Thanh-Huy Nguyen, Le Thien Phuc Nguyen, Quan Nguyen, and Ulas Bagci*

SCOPE: Label Extraction of Stroke Diagnosis from Unstructured Medical Reports Using Retrieval-Augmented Generation ......................... 10
*Mumu Aktar, Gunjan Jindal, Salome Lou Bosshart, Alexander Stebner, Pedro Paiva, Mariana Bento, Johanna Ospel, and Roberto Souza*

Mind the Evaluation Gap: Large Language Models for Structured Data Extraction from Radiology Reports ..................................... 19
*Amirhossein Sabour, Kailin Chu, Mehrdad Eshraghi Dehaghani, and Mehdi Moradi*

NeuroReport-MS: Multi-scale Agentic AI for Automated Clinical Report Generation in Multiple Sclerosis ........................................ 28
*Khaoula Alaoui Belghiti, Nour Eddine Zekaoui, Mounia Mikram, and Maryem Rhanoui*

REMix: Refinement-Enhanced Visual-Textual Mixing for Lesion Segmentation ....................................................... 36
*Soojin Hwang, Jaeyoon Sim, and Won Hwa Kim*

An LLM-Based Active Assistant and Smart Manual for CT Imaging Workflows ........................................................ 45
*Zeinab Aliakbari Mamaghani, Linda Vorberg, Andreas Maier, Alexander Katzmann, and Oliver Taubmann*

SIGMA: Auto-Regressive VLM for Automated Radiology Report Generation from Longitudinal 3D CT Volumes .......................... 53
*Khang C. Nguyen, Cheng Wang, Zong X. Shi, Yue Heng, Chuan Y. Qi, Masahiro Oda, and Kensaku Mori*

Specialised or Generic? Tokenization Choices for Radiology Language Models ........................................................... 62
*Hermione Warr, Wentian Xu, Harry Anthony, Yasin Ibrahim, Daniel R. McGowan, and Konstantinos Kamnitsas*

SCOPE: Speech-Guided COllaborative PErception Framework
for Surgical Scene Segmentation . . . . . . . . . . . . . . . . . . . . . . . . . . . . . . . . . . . . . 71
   *Jecia Z. Y. Mao, Francis X. Creighton, Russell H. Taylor,
   and Manish Sahu*

Imagining Alternatives: Towards High-Resolution 3D Counterfactual
Medical Image Generation via Language Guidance . . . . . . . . . . . . . . . . . . . . . . . 79
   *Mohamed Mohamed, Brennan Nichyporuk, Douglas L. Arnold,
   and Tal Arbel*

Pixels Under Pressure: Exploring Fine-Tuning Paradigms for Foundation
Models in High-Resolution Medical Imaging . . . . . . . . . . . . . . . . . . . . . . . . . . . . 88
   *Zahra TehraniNasab, Amar Kumar, and Tal Arbel*

DeepGPT-DILI: Integrating Graph Convolutional Networks and Large
Language Model Embeddings for Accurate Drug-Induced Liver Injury
Prediction . . . . . . . . . . . . . . . . . . . . . . . . . . . . . . . . . . . . . . . . . . . . . . . . . . . . . . . . . . 98
   *Minh Huu Nhat Le, Uyen Khoi Minh Huynh, Hong Xuan Ong,
   Phat K. Huynh, Minh-Toan Dinh, Han Hong Huynh, Hien Quang Kha,
   Phat Ky Nguyen, Xuan-Loc Huynh, An Thuy Vo, Thanh-Minh Nguyen,
   Thanh-Huy Nguyen, Quan Nguyen, and Nguyen Quoc Khanh Le*

From Reports to Relations: Large Language Models for Knowledge Graph
Extraction in Digital Pathology . . . . . . . . . . . . . . . . . . . . . . . . . . . . . . . . . . . . . . . . 107
   *Karthik Prathaban, Farhan Akram, Stefan Klein,
   and Martijn P. A. Starmans*

3D Vision–Language Models with Segmentation-Guided Multimodal
Data for Spinal MRI Report Generation . . . . . . . . . . . . . . . . . . . . . . . . . . . . . . . . 115
   *Hoda Helmy, Abdullah Hosseini, Ahmed Ibrahim, Asfand Baig-Mirza,
   Ahmed-Ramadan Sadek, and Ahmed Serag*

**Author Index** . . . . . . . . . . . . . . . . . . . . . . . . . . . . . . . . . . . . . . . . . . . . . . . . . . . . . 123

# GMAT: Grounded Multi-agent Clinical Description Generation for Text Encoder in Vision-Language MIL for Whole Slide Image Classification

Ngoc Bui Lam Quang[1](✉), Nam Le Nguyen Binh[1], Thanh-Huy Nguyen[2], Le Thien Phuc Nguyen[3], Quan Nguyen[4], and Ulas Bagci[5]

[1] AI VIETNAM, HANOI, Vietnam
ngoc.bui150019@vnuk.edu.vn
[2] Carnegie Mellon University, Pittsburgh, USA
[3] University of Wisconsin-Madison, Madison, USA
[4] PTIT, Hanoi, Vietnam
[5] Northwestern University, Evanston, USA

**Abstract.** Multiple Instance Learning (MIL) is the leading approach for whole slide image (WSI) classification, enabling efficient analysis of gigapixel pathology slides. Recent work has introduced vision-language models (VLMs) into MIL pipelines to incorporate medical knowledge through text-based class descriptions rather than simple class names. However, when these methods rely on large language models (LLMs) to generate clinical descriptions or use fixed-length prompts to represent complex pathology concepts, the limited token capacity of VLMs often constrains the expressiveness and richness of the encoded class information. Additionally, descriptions generated solely by LLMs may lack domain grounding and fine-grained medical specificity, leading to suboptimal alignment with visual features. To address these challenges, we propose a vision-language MIL framework with two key contributions: **(1) A grounded multi-agent description generation system** that leverages curated pathology textbooks and agent specialization (e.g., morphology, spatial context) to produce accurate and diverse clinical descriptions; **(2) A text encoding strategy using a list of descriptions** rather than a single prompt, capturing fine-grained and complementary clinical signals for better alignment with visual features. Integrated into a VLM-MIL pipeline, our approach shows improved performance over single-prompt class baselines and achieves results comparable to state-of-the-art models, as demonstrated on renal and lung cancer datasets.

**Keywords:** Multi-agent Systems · Whole Slide Images (WSIs) · Multiple Instance Learning (MIL) · Vision-Language Models (VLM)

---

N. B. L. Quang and N. Le N. Binh—Equal contribution.

# 1 Introduction

Pathological examination of tissue slides remains the gold standard for cancer diagnosis, offering high-resolution insights into cellular and structural abnormalities. However, whole slide images (WSIs) are gigapixel in size and contain complex, heterogeneous tissue patterns, making manual review labor-intensive and prone to variability.

To address the scale and complexity of WSIs, Multiple Instance Learning (MIL) has become the dominant approach for weakly supervised classification. In this framework, a slide is treated as a bag of image patches (instances), with supervision provided only at the slide level. Early models like ABMIL [1], CLAM [2], and TransMIL [3] leverage attention- or transformer-based aggregation to summarize patch features effectively. More recent work introduces advanced architectures, including HIPT [4] with hierarchical transformers, DSMIL [5] with dual-stream learning, and others such as CAMIL [6], DTFD-MIL [7], SNUFFY [8], and DGMIL [9], each proposing novel strategies for aggregation or feature modeling to improve classification performance.

Vision-Language Models (VLMs) such as CLIP have been incorporated into MIL pipelines to improve classification and interpretability by aligning visual features with textual prompts like disease labels or descriptive phrases. A common strategy involves prompt tuning, using either handcrafted or LLM-generated prompts. MGPath [10] introduces a multi-granular prompt framework that adapts across tissue magnifications to support few-shot learning. ViLaMIL [11] integrates magnification-aware embeddings with hierarchical attention across patch scales. MSCPT [12] proposes a multi-scale, context-aware prompt tuning method that aligns vision-text embeddings across magnifications. These approaches highlight the potential of multiscale integration and prompt design in enhancing VLM-based WSI classification. These works underscore the role of prompt design and scale integration in advancing VLM-based digital pathology. Building on this, recent efforts are now leveraging foundation models to further extend vision-language and vision-only capabilities.

Recent progress in Whole Slide Imaging (WSI) has been driven by Vision-Language Models (VLMs) like BioCLIP [13], PLIP [14], and CONCH [15], which align images with text for zero-shot performance. Dual-scale models such as ViLa-MIL [16] enhance fine-grained reasoning. In parallel, vision-only models like CTransPath [17] and GigaPath [18] learn strong representations without text, enabling scalable classification in low-label settings.

Recent vision-language models (VLMs) have shown promising alignment between images and text, but typically rely on generic prompts that may not fully capture the clinical detail needed in computational pathology. This can make it challenging to represent the subtle, fine-grained patterns found in whole slide images (WSIs), especially in complex diagnostic settings. To support more clinically informed prompting, we propose the **Grounded Multi-Agent Text Generation (GMAT)** framework, which generates descriptive class texts using structured knowledge from pathology textbooks. At its core is **GMATG**, a lightweight, modular component that coordinates a set of simple, role-specific agents to guide the description process. While GMATG does not use advanced agent architectures, it provides a practical workflow for incorporating domain-specific information into text generation. **GMAT** integrates GMATG into a vision-language MIL pipeline to enhance both performance. In summary, our approach introduces two key innovations:

- A multi-agent system for generating clinically grounded descriptions, where each agent focuses on a distinct pathological attribute (e.g., cellular morphology, tissue architecture), enabling comprehensive and structured knowledge extraction;
- A list-based text encoding strategy that replaces single-text prompts with multiple, diverse descriptions, capturing finer semantic details and improving alignment with visual features.

We integrate our approach into a vision-language MIL pipeline and demonstrate its effectiveness on renal and lung cancer datasets

## 2 Methodology

**Overview.** Our approach combines text-driven supervision with weakly supervised learning for WSI classification. It consists of two components: (1) **GMATG**, a multi-agent system that generates clinically grounded descriptions for each class, and (2) **GMAT**, a vision-language MIL model that aligns image patches with these descriptions using the CONCH encoder. Patch-level similarities are computed and aggregated using attention to produce slide-level predictions.

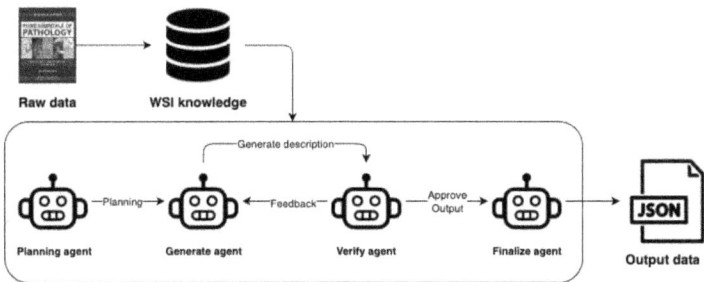

**Fig. 1.** Overview of GMATG. A team of specialized agents generates class-specific descriptions from domain knowledge, covering morphological, molecular, and clinical aspects. These are combined into rich text embeddings to guide visual understanding.

## 2.1 Grounded Multi-agent Text Generation (GMATG)

To support class-specific description generation, we first build a structured knowledge base by extracting relevant disease-specific content from curated pathology textbooks, as shown in Figure 1. This serves as a shared foundation for all agents in the system, enabling consistent and medically grounded output.

The agents in this system, which could be powered by an advanced model like Gemini 2.5-Pro, perform distinct roles:

- **Planning Agent:** Creates a detailed guide for describing a specific cancer, outlining structure, rules for analyzing cell and tissue features, required clinical information, and quality standards. The output is a markdown plan with a summary, analysis instructions, and validation steps to guide the other agents.
- **Generate Agent:** Uses the plan and shared knowledge base to compose an initial draft of the class description.
- **Verify Agent:** Reviews the written description for medical accuracy, completeness, and consistent terminology based on pathology standards. It produces a corrected version with a quality report and recommendations for improvement.
- **Finalize Agent:** Converts the approved description into a structured JSON file, using the cancer type as the main key and a list of short clinical sentences as values. These are ordered from general to microscopic, molecular, and clinical details. The agent ensures proper formatting, concise language, and removes all markdown.

Overall, this multi-agent workflow ensures structured planning, generation, and review of each class description. By combining expert-curated knowledge with specialized agent roles, GMATG generates clinically grounded, semantically rich prompts for downstream vision-language MIL classification (Fig 2).

## 2.2 Vision-Language MIL Classification

Our model, **GMAT**, uses a vision-language architecture with CONCH as a shared encoder for both image patches and text descriptions. Each whole slide image (WSI) is divided into patches at 5× and 10× magnification, which are processed by the CONCH visual encoder and mapped into a shared embedding space. For the text branch, we use multiple class-specific descriptions generated by GMATG. Stored in JSON format, these prompts capture diverse pathological features for each class. Each description is tokenized and encoded using the frozen CONCH text encoder to produce normalized text embeddings.

To align image and text, we compute the similarity between each patch embedding and all description embeddings. These per-patch similarity scores are aggregated into class-level scores by averaging over the descriptions corresponding to each class. Finally, we apply an attention-based aggregation mechanism, adapted from the CLAM model, to weight and combine patch-level class

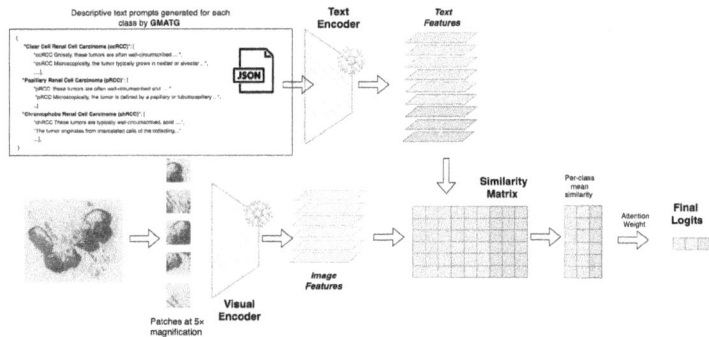

**Fig. 2. Overview of our MIL framework for 5× magnification.** Patch features at 5× magnification are embedded using the CONCH visual encoder and matched with GMAT-generated text descriptions. Similarity scores are computed via visual-text alignment and aggregated using soft attention to produce class logits. Features from 10× magnification are processed in parallel, and predictions from both scales are fused for final slide-level classification.

scores. This results in a slide-level prediction, trained using cross-entropy loss. The overall architecture is illustrated in 2.

## 3 Experiment

### 3.1 Datasets

We evaluate on two cancer subtyping datasets: **TCGA-RCC (Renal)** with WSIs from Clear Cell (KIRC), Papillary (KIRP), and Chromophobe (KICH) subtypes, and **TCGA-Lung** with WSIs for Lung Adenocarcinoma (LUAD) and Lung Squamous Cell Carcinoma (LUSC). Both datasets use patient-level splits to prevent data leakage.

### 3.2 Methods Under Comparision

We evaluate zero-shot and fine-tuned performance across multiple settings. For zero-shot, we assess CONCH using either a single-description setup (denoted as *Single Class Description* in the table) or a list of GMATG-generated descriptions. The single-description setup follows the two-level prompt format from ViLa-MIL [16], covering 5× and 10× magnifications. For fine-tuning, we compare ViLa-MIL with standard prompts to our GMAT framework. All methods use the same CONCH encoder for both text and image to ensure fairness. An ablation study further examines the impact of the multi-agent design versus a single-agent variant.

## 3.3 Result and Analysis

First, we evaluate the effectiveness of our approach in a zero-shot setting using the CONCH model. Specifically, we compare performance using a single class description versus a list of descriptions generated by GMATG. For the class description baseline, we adopt the two-level prompt structure used in ViLa-MIL [16]. In contrast, the list-based variant includes multiple, structured descriptions per class, covering diverse pathological aspects. Results show that the list-based approach consistently improves AUC, F1 score across both TCGA-RCC and TCGA-Lung datasets.

**Table 1. Zero-shot and Fine-tuned Performance on TCGA-RCC (Test Set)**
List-based descriptions are generated by the GMATG framework.

| Model | Description Type | AUC (↑) | F1 Score (↑) | Accuracy (↑) |
|---|---|---|---|---|
| Zero-shot Setting | | | | |
| CONCH | Single Class Description | 0.5730 ± 0.0314 | 0.3466 ± 0.0138 | 0.4821 ± 0.0070 |
| CONCH | **List from GMATG** | **0.5912 ± 0.0328** | **0.3691 ± 0.0347** | 0.4357 ± 0.0514 |
| Fine-tuned Setting | | | | |
| ViLa-MIL | Single Class Description | 0.9844 ± 0.0070 | 0.9028 ± 0.0445 | 0.9197 ± 0.0184 |
| GMAT | **List from GMATG** | 0.9791 ± 0.0116 | **0.9131 ± 0.0293** | **0.9262 ± 0.0294** |

**Table 2. Zero-shot and Fine-tuned Performance on TCGA-Lung (Test Set)**
List-based descriptions are generated by the GMATG framework.

| Model | Description Type | AUC (↑) | F1 Score (↑) | Accuracy (↑) |
|---|---|---|---|---|
| Zero-shot Setting | | | | |
| CONCH | Single Class Description | 0.6767 ± 0.0288 | 0.6116 ± 0.0164 | 0.6300 ± 0.0089 |
| CONCH | **List from GMATG** | **0.7226 ± 0.0233** | **0.6693 ± 0.0262** | **0.6711 ± 0.0247** |
| Fine-tuned Setting | | | | |
| ViLa-MIL | Single Class Description | 0.9499 ± 0.0308 | 0.8894 ± 0.0418 | 0.8899 ± 0.0422 |
| GMAT | **List from GMATG** | **0.9641 ± 0.0057** | **0.9023 ± 0.0184** | **0.9028 ± 0.0183** |

We evaluate both zero-shot and fine-tuned performance on TCGA-RCC 1 and TCGA-Lung 2, comparing standard class-level descriptions with our list-based prompts generated by GMATG.

**Zero-Shot.** In the zero-shot setting, GMATG consistently improves performance over single-class descriptions. The improvements are especially notable on TCGA-Lung, where AUC rises from 0.6767 to 0.7226, along with gains in F1 and accuracy. This suggests that GMATG provides more informative and discriminative prompts, even without fine-tuning.

**Fine-Tuned.** With fine-tuning, GMAT achieves comparable performance ViLa-MIL on both datasets. On TCGA-RCC, it shows slight improvements in F1 and accuracy. On TCGA-Lung, GMAT achieves better results across all metrics, demonstrating the value of its structured, multi-agent descriptions during training (Table 4).

Overall, GMAT achieves performance comparable to existing approaches in both zero-shot and fine-tuned settings, highlighting the potential of using richer, clinically grounded prompts (Table 3).

### 3.4 Ablation

To evaluate the impact of the multi-agent design in GMATG, we compare it with a simpler single-agent version. In the single-agent setting, one agent extracts text from pathology textbooks and creates a list of class-specific descriptions without help or feedback from other agents. While it still uses a list-based approach, it lacks the structured, collaborative process of GMATG.

**Table 3. Ablation Study on TCGA-RCC**

| Model Variant | AUC (↑) | F1 Score (↑) | Accuracy (↑) |
|---|---|---|---|
| Single Agent | 0.9776 ± 0.0109 | 0.9124 ± 0.0296 | 0.9239 ± 0.0304 |
| Multi-Agent (GMATG) | **0.9791 ± 0.0116** | **0.9131 ± 0.0293** | **0.9262 ± 0.0294** |

**Table 4. Ablation Study on TCGA-Lung**

| Model Variant | AUC (↑) | F1 Score (↑) | Accuracy (↑) |
|---|---|---|---|
| Single Agent | 0.9615 ± 0.0056 | 0.8968 ± 0.0145 | 0.8976 ± 0.0142 |
| Multi-Agent (GMATG) | **0.9641 ± 0.0057** | **0.9023 ± 0.0184** | **0.9028 ± 0.0183** |

As shown in the ablation results for TCGA-RCC 3 and TCGA-Lung 4, the multi-agent system performs slightly better across all metrics. This suggests that having multiple agents working together leads to more accurate and comprehensive descriptions.

## 4 Conclusion

We presented **GMAT**, a framework for vision-language MIL that generates clinically grounded, list-based prompts using a multi-agent system. By drawing from pathology textbooks, GMAT captures diverse and structured descriptions that align more effectively with visual features. Experiments on TCGA-RCC and TCGA-Lung show consistent improvements in both zero-shot and fine-tuned settings. These results highlight the value of domain-informed, collaborative prompt generation for enhancing performance and interpretability in computational pathology.

**Acknowledgement.** We would like to thank AI VIETNAM for facilitating computational resources.

# References

1. Ilse, M., Tomczak, J., Welling, M.: Attention-based deep multiple instance learning, In: International Conference on Machine Learning, pp. 2127–2136, PMLR (2018)
2. Lu, M.Y., Williamson, D.F., Chen, T.Y., Chen, R.J., Barbieri, M., Mahmood, F.: Data-efficient and weakly supervised computational pathology on whole-slide images. Nat. Biomed. Eng. **5**(6), 555–570 (2021)
3. Shao, Z., Bian, H., Chen, Y., Wang, Y., Zhang, J., Ji, X., et al.: Transmil: transformer based correlated multiple instance learning for whole slide image classification. Adv. Neural. Inf. Process. Syst. **34**, 2136–2147 (2021)
4. Chen, R.J., et al.: Scaling vision transformers to gigapixel images via hierarchical self-supervised learning,' In: Proceedings of the IEEE/CVF Conference on Computer Vision and Pattern Recognition, pp. 16144–16155 (2022)
5. Li, B., Li, Y., Eliceiri, K.W.: Dual-stream multiple instance learning network for whole slide image classification with self-supervised contrastive learning, In: Proceedings of the IEEE/CVF Conference on Computer Vision and Pattern Recognition, pp. 14318–14328 (2021)
6. Fourkioti, O., De Vries, M., Bakal, C.: CAMIL: context-aware multiple instance learning for cancer detection and subtyping in whole slide images, In: The Twelfth International Conference on Learning Representations (2024)
7. Zhang, H., et al.: DTFD-MIL: Double-tier feature distillation multiple instance learning for histopathology whole slide image classification.
8. Jafarinia, H., Alipanah, A., Razavi, S., Mirzaie, N., Rohban, M.H.: Snuffy: Efficient whole slide image classifier (2024)
9. Qu, L., Luo, X., Liu, S., Wang, M., Song, Z.: Dgmil: distribution guided multiple instance learning for whole slide image classification, In: International Conference on Medical Image Computing and Computer-assisted Intervention, pp. 24–34, Springer (2022)
10. Nguyen, A.-T., et al.: Mgpath: vision-language model with multi-granular prompt learning for few-shot WSI classification (2025)
11. Nguyen, A.-T., et al.: Few-shot whole slide pathology classification with multi-granular vision-language models, In: ICLR 2025 Workshop on Foundation Models in the Wild (2025)
12. Han, M., Qu, L., Yang, D., Zhang, X., Wang, X., Zhang, L.: Mscpt: few-shot whole slide image classification with multi-scale and context-focused prompt tuning, IEEE Transactions on Medical Imaging, pp. 1–1 (2025)
13. Zhang, S., et al.: Biomedclip: a multimodal biomedical foundation model pretrained from fifteen million scientific image-text pairs, arXiv preprint arXiv:2403.xxxxx (2024)

14. Huang, Z., Bianchi, F., Yuksekgonul, M., Montine, T.J., Zou, J.: A visual-language foundation model for pathology image analysis using medical twitter. Nat. Med. **29**(9), 2307–2316 (2023)
15. Lu, M.Y., et al.: Visual language pretrained multiple instance zero-shot transfer for histopathology images, In: Proceedings of the IEEE/CVF Conference on Computer Vision and Pattern Recognition, pp. 19764–19775 (2023)
16. Shi, J., Li, C., Gong, T., Zheng, Y., Fu, H.: Vila-mil: Dual-scale vision-language multiple instance learning for whole slide image classification, In: Proceedings of the IEEE/CVF Conference on Computer Vision and Pattern Recognition, pp. 11248–11258 (2024)
17. Wang, X., et al.: Transformer-based unsupervised contrastive learning for histopathological image classification. Med. Image Anal. **81**, 102559 (2022)
18. Xu, H., et al.: A whole-slide foundation model for digital pathology from real-world data, Nature, pp. 1–8 (2024)

# SCOPE: Label Extraction of Stroke Diagnosis from Unstructured Medical Reports Using Retrieval-Augmented Generation

Mumu Aktar[1]([✉]), Gunjan Jindal[1,2], Salome Lou Bosshart[3], Alexander Stebner[3], Pedro Paiva[1], Mariana Bento[1], Johanna Ospel[1], and Roberto Souza[1]

[1] University of Calgary, Calgary, Alberta, Canada
mumu.aktar@ucalgary.ca
[2] Foothills medical centre, Calgary, Alberta, Canada
[3] University Hospital Basel, Basel, Switzerland

**Abstract.** Big data research in neuroradiology relies on labeled datasets, often extracted manually from imaging in a time- and labor-intensive process. Although artificial intelligence (AI) advances automated analysis, security concerns limit the sharing of medical images. Radiology reports offer an alternative but require manual labeling. AI-assisted labeling could be beneficial, but privacy risks arise with cloud-based tools such as ChatGPT, and many AI models lack specialized development for neuroimaging. We propose SCOPE (Stroke COntent Parsing and Extraction), a novel approach that combines an open-source large language model (Llama-3.1) and retrieval-augmented generation (RAG) to extract stroke diagnosis labels from medical reports. This method generates labeled datasets linked to patient imaging data for clinical research. Leveraging a pre-trained Llama model with RAG eliminates the need for fine-tuning (i.e., re-training) and allows seamless data expansion. With an overall accuracy of 0.93, a sensitivity of 0.92, a specificity value of 0.96, and an F1-score of 0.95, SCOPE outperforms Llama-3.1 without RAG and Llama-3.1 with fine-tuning. The GitHub code is available: https://github.com/mumuaktar/SCOPE/.

**Keywords:** RAG · Label extraction · Stroke diagnosis · LLM

## 1 Introduction

Researchers in the field of neurosciences, and stroke researchers specifically, often rely on data from labeled radiology reports. This is especially true for large, multi-jurisdictional datasets where pooling imaging data is challenging or impossible, or when privacy and security concerns restrict access. Extraction of significant label information, such as patient diagnosis, from unstructured radiology reports (which are still common practice in many neuroradiology departments) is, however, cumbersome and time-consuming. This task becomes even more challenging when the specific information a researcher is looking for is not explicitly mentioned in the report or is phrased differently. For instance, extracting a patient's age can be as simple as a keyword search. However, extracting labels such as "acute ischemic stroke", which depend on multiple criteria (i.e., the presence of occlusion on CT angiography in the context of early ischemic changes on non-contrast CT), is much harder to perform manually. The workload increases significantly when extracting information from a large set of medical reports, rendering manual efforts both impractical and inefficient. Large language models (LLMs) offer a promising solution for handling large sets of text data and extracting critical information from unstructured medical reports. Recently, models such as GPT-4 [1] and Llama3 [2] have gained popularity for these tasks. A recent study by Fink et al. [3] has proven that GPT-4 [1] outperformed ChatGPT in data mining and labeling oncologic phenotypes in lung cancer from medical reports with 96% accuracy. However, privacy concerns arise when using commercial models like GPT-4 [1], as they may inadvertently expose sensitive patient details. In such cases, open-source LLMs that can be deployed locally, like the widely used Llama [4], are better suited for ensuring data security. Llama3 [2], developed by Meta AI, is a transformer-based model pre-trained on a diverse domain of text data and capable of generating contextually relevant text based on specific instructions. A significant issue with directly using Llama3 [2] in the medical context is its tendency to "hallucinate" (produce incorrect or fabricated outputs) since it has been trained on a broader set of datasets rather than one tailored to the medical, let alone the neuroradiological, domain. To address this, an in-house LLM (for example, BURExtractLlama [5], Me-Llama [6], medLlama [7]) can be used to fine-tune the model on custom medical/neuroradiological datasets. However, the domain-specific nature of fine-tuning is limited by the lack of large, labeled, and imbalanced datasets. Additionally, in the healthcare domain, where reports are dynamic and ever-evolving, pre-fine-tuned LLMs might miss critical new information, a significant concern in medical applications. To address these limitations, retrieval-augmented generation (RAG) [8] can be integrated with Llama3 [2] to enhance its performance, particularly in domain-specific tasks. In this framework, the retrieval component allows the model to access an up-to-date, external knowledge base such as documents detailing stroke diagnosis and extract relevant information. The generator component then produces responses based on both the user query and the retrieved content. By incorporating RAG [8], the Llama3 [2] model can generate contextually informed outputs while mitigating the limitations of outdated or incomplete internal knowledge. MEDRAG, a RAG toolkit for answering medical questions introduced in the study by Xiong et al. [9], demonstrated that integrating RAG [8] with various Llama models improved accuracy by up to 18%. Therefore, we focused on extracting the stroke diagnosis labels from the medical reports with our proposed model, SCOPE, which combines Llama3.1 [2] with RAG [8].

## 2 Dataset Description

For the task of label extraction, the "Optimizing Imaging for Medium Vessel Occlusion Stroke" (ESCAPE-OPTIMUS) dataset was utilized (REB 23-0291), a retrospective multi-center cohort study that includes all patients who received a CT head and neck angiogram at any imaging facility in the province of Alberta, Canada, between April 1, 2022, and June 30, 2023. The dataset includes clinical information from several administrative databases, including discharge diagnosis codes and procedure codes for all treatments administered within the respective episode of care during which the head CT and neck angiogram were obtained. This includes acute ischemic stroke treatments such as intravenous thrombolysis and mechanical thrombectomy. Since head CT and neck angiography are standard for suspected acute ischemic stroke in all Albertan medical facilities—and are also used for other conditions like blunt cerebrovascular injury, carotid artery stenting follow-up, and pre-cardiac surgery workup—the dataset includes both acute and non-acute stroke cases. For the current study, an expert-labeled subset of 628 randomly chosen medical reports, along with their ground truth labels, was used. The data was labeled by a stroke neurologist and board-certified radiologists in neuroradiology training who were instructed by a fellowship-trained neuroradiologist and consulted the neuroradiologist in doubtful cases.

## 3 Methodology

The proposed approach, SCOPE, combines an RAG [8] strategy with the Llama3.1 model [2]. In this framework, an external document database is used as a knowledge base, and domain-specific information is retrieved and provided to the Llama3.1 [2] model alongside the processed radiology report. The model then generates a response based on a specific query, guided by a detailed set of criteria defined in a custom system prompt. Since the Llama model [2] is already pre-trained on a broad, general-purpose corpus, and the RAG [8] framework allows for the integration of domain-specific knowledge related to stroke, our approach does not require additional training. As a result, SCOPE operates in a zero-shot or inference-only setting and is used directly for testing and evaluation without further fine-tuning. The overall methodology of SCOPE is shown in Fig. 1.

### 3.1 Preprocessing Reports

Since medical reports are typically unstructured, the first step in the pipeline involves converting each report into a standard format, independent of clinical documentation styles. To enable effective retrieval and generation, two automated preprocessing steps are applied to each report before it is incorporated into the RAG+Llama3 pipeline for testing. Initially, a medical report was cleaned, removing the irrelevant information (for example, procedure date, dictation date, transcription date, electronic signature date, order, and accession numbers). Additionally, to ensure consistency and improve the interpretability of

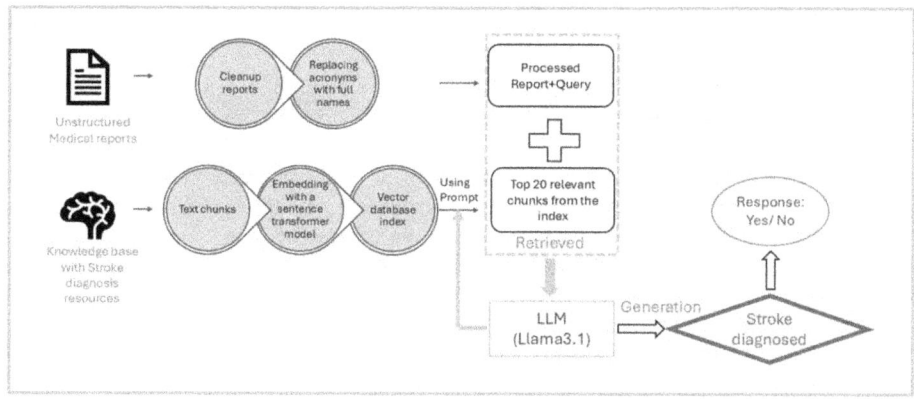

**Fig. 1.** Overall methodology of SCOPE.

the reports, the common acronyms used in CT head and neck angiograms (e.g., anterior cerebral artery (ACA), middle cerebral artery (MCA), posterior cerebral artery (PCA), basilar artery (BA), internal carotid artery (ICA), vertebral artery (VA)) which were used in some reports, were replaced with the spelled out versions of these terms.

### 3.2 Generation of Knowledge-Base and Query Response

To construct the knowledge base for the RAG setting in our SCOPE pipeline, we gathered relevant information from 13 foundational stroke-related research articles published in two peer-reviewed journals (Stroke[1] and Journal of Stroke[2]), as well as from a glossary of stroke terms[3], and a curated PDF containing stroke-related content from Wikipedia. This helps the model to answer domain-specific queries since Llama3.1 [2] is pre-trained on a broad dataset. We preprocessed external documents by removing non-informative sections (e.g., conclusion, acknowledgment, references, and bibliography) and segmenting the remaining text into 1,000 character-based chunks using a CharacterTextSplitter. This chunking strategy improves retrieval performance by creating manageable passages that align with the RAG paradigm. Furthermore, a document encoder (all-MiniLM-L6-v2 from Hugging Face) was used to convert the chunks into numerical embeddings, mapping each chunk to a vector in a high-dimensional space. This allowed the model to understand the context and relationships between different content, making similar content represented by similar vectors. At query time, a query engine was used to retrieve the top 20 most relevant chunks based on cosine similarity between the query embedding and document embedding. These retrieved chunks, along with the processed report, were then passed to

---

[1] https://www.ahajournals.org/journal/str.
[2] https://www.j-stroke.org/.
[3] https://www.med.umich.edu/1libr/Stroke/StrokeGlossary.pdf.

the Llama3.1 [2] model for final response generation, guided by a system prompt shown below.

### System Prompt

```
You are a Retrieval-Augmented Generation (RAG) system tasked with
    analyzing a medical report to determine whether the patient has
    been diagnosed with an acute or subacute stroke. Consider the
    presence of conditions like the following as evidence for
    stroke:
-Acute or subacute ischemia
-Acute or subacute Cerebral/Lentiform/Insular/Cortical/Cerebellar/
    internal capsule infarction (or infarct)
-Left/right middle cerebral artery/territory or M2 branch occlusion
-Hemorrhage
-Sudden and acute or subacute neurological symptoms like loss of
    gray, white, wedge-shaped area of hypodensity, based on the
    report, only if they lead to acute or subacute stroke
-Early ischemic change
-Acute or subacute (anterior / middle / posterior / basilar /
    carotid / vertebral artery) occlusion
-Acute or subacute (anterior / middle / posterior / basilar /
    carotid / vertebral artery) thrombus
-Acute or subacute (anterior / middle / posterior / basilar /
    carotid / vertebral artery) embolus
If the report does not show evidence of such an acute or subacute
    event, respond with 'No' and provide a brief explanation. If
    the report indicates a stroke, respond with 'Yes' and provide
    evidence of the acute or subacute event(s).
Please ignore chronic conditions like chronic infarcts or old
    infarcts, as they do not indicate an acute/subacute stroke
    event. Be concise and specific. If you are uncertain about any
    report, say 'No', focusing solely on acute or subacute stroke-
    related events.
```

This prompt was carefully structured to emphasize key radiological terms and patterns associated with acute and subacute cerebrovascular events. Explicitly detailing anatomical and pathological descriptors—such as "acute or subacute cerebral/lentiform/insular/cortical/cerebellar/internal capsule infarction," and "anterior, middle, posterior, basilar, carotid, or vertebral artery" occlusion, embolus, or thrombus-consistently guided the model toward more accurate extraction of stroke diagnosis labels based on critical criteria identified in the reports.

## 4 Experimental Setup

To generate responses based on specific queries using SCOPE, Meta Llama 3.1 8B Instruct model[4] was used as the core language model. To reduce memory consumption and accelerate inference, the model was loaded with 4-bit quantization using the NF4 quantization scheme. This configuration also employed double quantization and half-precision floating-point computation (float16), allowing the model to operate efficiently on limited hardware while preserving performance. LoRA was applied to key transformer components, including attention and projection layers, with a low-rank value of 4 and a scaling factor of 16. The model was instantiated with a context window of 4,096 tokens, allowing it to process long sequences of retrieved information along with the input query. The maximum length of generated text was capped at 256 tokens to ensure concise and focused responses.

The performance of our method, SCOPE, is validated using a test set comprising 406 stroke cases and 222 non-stroke case patients' reports in one experiment. We evaluated our proposed method's performance by comparing the predicted stroke diagnosis labels of the reports to the ground truth labels scored by the radiologists. To evaluate the effectiveness of integrating RAG [8] with the Llama3.1 [2] model, we compared the performance of SCOPE against the direct use of pre-trained Llama3.1 [2] (without RAG). Additionally, we conducted fine-tuning of the pre-trained Llama 3.1 [2] model on our dataset to establish a performance baseline under supervised training conditions. For the fine-tuning experiment, all 628 labeled reports were split into training and testing sets, with 70% used for training (including a 15% validation split) and the remaining 30% used as the test set. To ensure a fair comparison across methods, the performance of the fine-tuned model, SCOPE, and the direct use of the pre-trained Llama 3.1 model without RAG were evaluated using the same 30% test set in another experiment.

## 5 Results

To evaluate the performance of SCOPE, a total of 628 reports were considered. An overall accuracy of 0.93 with a sensitivity of 0.92 (patients diagnosed with stroke, labeled as 1), a specificity of 0.96, and an F1-score of 0.95 are obtained by the proposed pipeline (Confusion Matrix in Table 1). Table 2 presents the performance comparison between SCOPE, pre-trained Llama3.1 only (without integrating RAG), and fine-tuned Llama3.1 on our dataset. From Table 2, it can be seen that our method demonstrates superior performance compared to others in stroke diagnosis label extraction. Adding RAG to Llama3.1 improved its sensitivity by 4% on this test dataset. Note that SCOPE was previously evaluated on the full dataset (Table 1); further, its performance is re-evaluated specifically on the held-out 30% test set for consistency (Table 2).

---

[4] https://huggingface.co/meta-llama/Llama-3.1-8B-Instruct.

**Table 1.** Confusion Matrix of Predictions Evaluated Using SCOPE.

| Actual / Predicted | Predicted Positive | Predicted Negative |
|---|---|---|
| Actual Positive | 374 (TP) | 32 (FN) |
| Actual Negative | 10 (FP) | 212 (TN) |

**Table 2.** Performance comparison of SCOPE with other methods.

| Metric | SCOPE | LLaMA3.1 (Pre-trained) | LLaMA3.1 (Fine-tuned) |
|---|---|---|---|
| Accuracy | 0.97 | 0.95 | 0.94 |
| Sensitivity | 0.97 | 0.93 | 0.91 |
| F1-Score | 0.97 | 0.96 | 0.95 |

## 6 Discussion

This study presents SCOPE, a novel approach for the automated extraction of clinical and imaging information of CT head and neck angiograms from unstructured radiological reports. The tool showed a sensitivity of 0.92 and a specificity of 0.96 in extracting acute ischemic stroke labels. This efficient data extraction tool has the potential to streamline stroke research with large datasets, eliminating the need for time- and labor-intensive manual data extraction from radiology reports. As the tool can be applied offline on local servers, thus avoiding uploading critical medical information into cloud-based AI tools like ChatGPT, it complies with common data security concerns regarding sensitive medical data. Although the proposed model in this pilot study was implemented for acute ischemic stroke diagnosis labels' extraction only, tuning the system prompt based on researchers' needs, other stroke-specific information, e.g. the type and size of vessel occlusion (large vessel occlusion in the terminal internal carotid artery and M1 segment vs. medium-sized vessel occlusion in the distal M2 segment and beyond), new or evolving ischemic changes, old infarcts, chronic vessel occlusions, artery stenosis, intracranial hemorrhage etc. could potentially be extracted.

Since RAG does not require task-specific training, it leverages pre-trained language models and dynamically incorporates domain knowledge from curated sources at inference. This flexibility allows easy adaptation to other domains by updating reference documents and prompts, enabling structured information extraction without retraining.

To assess the performance of SCOPE, we compared its outputs to ground truth data that were acquired by expert radiologists through manual review of radiology reports. Following further validation, our goal is to deploy SCOPE to previously unlabeled reports within the dataset, automating the extraction of critical diagnostic labels and eliminating the need for manual annotation. Furthermore, these automatically extracted labels could be linked to imaging data, addressing the limitations of manually curated ground truth and enabling downstream applications such as supervised learning, where large, consistently labeled datasets are essential.

Looking ahead, our knowledge base could potentially be enhanced by incorporating additional information from other sources, for example, PubMed. Furthermore, we could explore an alternative RAG architecture proposed by Jiang et al. [10]. Although Llama3.1 [2] has shown strong efficacy, exploring other state-of-the-art LLMs such as PMC-Llama [11], which is fine-tuned in medical documents, could help reduce the false negative rate observed in our work, thus minimizing the risk of missing cases with confirmed stroke.

# 7 Conclusion

Our novel SCOPE method uses RAG to automatically extract acute ischemic stroke diagnosis labels from unstructured CT angiogram reports, offering a scalable alternative to manual labeling. With a dynamic knowledge base, SCOPE can extend to other neuroradiology domains, enabling research when only radiology reports are available and imaging data is inaccessible.

**Acknowledgments.** Dr. Roberto Souza thanks NSERC for ongoing operating support for this project (RGPIN/2021-02858).

**Disclosure of Interests.** The authors have no competing interests to declare that are relevant to the content of this article.

# References

1. T. OpenAI et al.: GPT-4 Technical Report. arXiv preprint arXiv:2303.08774 (2023)
2. Grattafiori, A., Dubey, A., Jauhri, A., et al.: The LLaMA 3 Herd of Models. arXiv preprint arXiv:2407.21783 (2024)
3. Fink, M.A., Bischoff, A., Fink, C.A., et al.: Potential of ChatGPT and GPT-4 for data mining of free-text CT reports on lung cancer. Radiology **308**(3), e231362 (2023)
4. Touvron, H., Lavril, T., Izacard, G., et al.: LLaMA: open and efficient foundation language models. arXiv preprint arXiv:2302.13971 (2023)
5. Chen, Y., Yang, H., Pan, H., et al.: BURExtract-Llama: an LLM for clinical concept extraction in breast ultrasound reports. In: Proceeding 1st Int. Workshop on Multimedia Computing for Health and Medicine, pp. 53–58 (2024)
6. Xie, Q., Chen, Q., Chen, A., et al.: Me LLaMA: foundation large language models for medical applications. arXiv preprint arXiv:2402.12749 (2024)
7. PAIXAI: Astrid-7B-LLama-Med. Hugging Face. https://huggingface.co/PAIXAI/Astrid-7B-LLama-Med. Accessed: 4 July 2024
8. Lewis, P., Perez, E., Piktus, A., et al.: Retrieval-augmented generation for knowledge-intensive NLP tasks. Adv. Neural. Inf. Process. Syst. **33**, 9459–9474 (2020)
9. Xiong, G., Jin, Q., Lu, Z., Zhang, A.: Benchmarking retrieval-augmented generation for medicine. arXiv preprint arXiv:2402.13178 (2024)

10. Jiang, Z., Xu, F.F., Gao, L., et al.: Active retrieval augmented generation. arXiv preprint arXiv:2305.06983 (2023)
11. Wu, C., Zhang, X., Zhang, Y., et al.: PMC-LLaMA: further finetuning LLaMA on medical papers. arXiv preprint arXiv:2304.14454 (2023)

# Mind the Evaluation Gap: Large Language Models for Structured Data Extraction from Radiology Reports

Amirhossein Sabour, Kailin Chu, Mehrdad Eshraghi Dehaghani, and Mehdi Moradi(✉)

McMaster University, Hamilton, ON, Canada
{saboua4,chuk20,eshragm,moradm4}@mcmaster.ca

**Abstract.** Extracting structured labels from free-text radiology reports is essential for building large-scale datasets used to train and evaluate models in medical AI. However, this process is costly, typically requiring expert annotators. Prior efforts often rely on noisy rule-based NLP or use LLMs without directly evaluating their structured data extraction capabilities. In this work, we address this evaluation gap by extensively benchmarking open-weight general and medical LLMs for extracting structured labels from chest X-ray (CXR) reports using a radiologist-verified dataset. We consider two tasks: (1) *Disease-Only* label extraction, and (2) *Location+Disease*, where each disease is paired with its anatomical region. We compare fine-tuning and in-context learning (ICL) across models ranging from 0.5B to 72B parameters. Our results show that a fine-tuned 7B model matches the performance of a 72B model in ICL mode. We advocate for rigorous and task-specific evaluation of LLMs in medical AI and highlight open-weight models as privacy-preserving, cost-effective, and clinically deployable solutions.

**Keywords:** Structured Radiology Report Extraction · Benchmarking · Open-weight Medical LLMs · Chest X-ray reporting

## 1 Introduction

One of the primary obstacles to integrating AI into radiology is the difficulty and high cost of producing high-quality labeled datasets. Historically, large-scale medical imaging datasets have leveraged radiology reports written during routine clinical care. Initial efforts produced large corpora of chest radiographs with corresponding labels, often relying on classical NLP methods, which can introduce

---

A. Sabour and K. Chu—Equal contribution.

considerable noise into the annotations [13]. Although later datasets adopted more refined labeling strategies [8], the resulting annotations, while sufficient for training large models, are not accurate enough to serve as ground truth. In contrast, the ImaGenome dataset [15], derived from MIMIC [9], includes a subset of images labeled through expert consensus by three radiologists. This "gold" dataset has primarily been used for model sanity checking and evaluation [3,12].

Transforming free-text radiology reports into structured object-attribute pairs is a fundamental step in utilizing large-scale clinical datasets. It supports model training, enables downstream applications, and has applications in systems for insurance, billing, auditing, and clinical decision support. However, this task typically requires domain experts, often board-certified radiologists or residents, making large-scale structured data extraction efforts prohibitively costly. Recently, large language models (LLMs) have emerged as a means to extract structured information from clinical text [2,6]. Commercial models, such as ChatGPT, have been used to structure radiology reports [4,5,11]. However, most prior works lack rigorous quantitative evaluation on this task; instead, they either assume the LLM outputs are "good enough" for their downstream task or validate them only using Med-QA benchmarks [1], which differ fundamentally from structured data extraction. This is a key shortcoming in the context of medical AI, where factual precision is non-negotiable. Furthermore, the use of commercial LLMs can raise ethical and legal concerns, which may deter adoption by the medical community. Sending sensitive patient data to external APIs can compromise privacy and risk unauthorized use, such as training proprietary models for commercial benefit. We argue that privacy-critical clinical applications should instead rely on open-weight, auditable LLMs that can be deployed locally. The study in [14] offers a useful starting point, but the evaluation is limited in scope and does not consider different model sizes or types, both of which are important for clinical deployment. In this work, we address these challenges, focusing on the task of structuring radiology reports using open-weight LLMs, and highlight the need for rigorous quantitative evaluation based on classification metrics. Specifically, we benchmark open-weight LLMs on two structured data extraction tasks from free-text chest X-ray (CXR) reports using the gold-labeled ImaGenome subset (i.e., radiologist-annotated data): (1) *Disease-Only*, where disease mentions are extracted from a free-text report, and (2) *Location+Disease*, where each disease and its spatial location are extracted. Although our experiments focus on CXR reports, the proposed methodology and evaluation framework are generalizable across imaging modalities and datasets. Our contributions are summarized below:

– **Comprehensive benchmarking of structured data extraction:** We evaluate general-purpose and medical-domain open-weight LLMs across model sizes from 0.5B to 72B parameters on both the *Disease-Only* and *Location+Disease* tasks by formulating them as classification problems and reporting standard metrics.
– **Fine-tuning vs. In-Context Learning:** We compare fine-tuning and in-context learning (ICL), showing that fine-tuning offers clear gains when

feasible, while ICL provides a viable alternative when compute or data constraints prevent fine-tuning.

We advocate for the use of open-weight LLMs in privacy-sensitive applications involving protected health information due to their local deployability, zero query cost, lack of reliance on external APIs, and higher likelihood of clinical adoption. Importantly, our goal is not to reestablish that fine-tuning outperforms ICL but to address the evaluation gap in using LLMs to process medical reports and quantitatively benchmark **open-weight LLMs on structured data extraction**, specifically object-attribute extraction from free-text radiology reports. LLM capabilities in structured medical data extraction **must be evaluated directly**, not just through subsequent downstream tasks. Code will be released publicly.

## 2 Methods

### 2.1 Problem Definition

Let $\mathcal{R}$ be a predefined set of anatomical regions and $\mathcal{A}$ a predefined set of diseases or attributes. Each free-text radiology report $T$ consists of one or more paragraphs detailing a radiologist's observations and interpretations of a CXR image $\mathbf{X}$. Each free-text report $T$ is associated with a corresponding structured report, represented by a set of region-attribute-presence labels, denoted as $\mathcal{Y} = \{(r, a, p) \mid r \in \mathcal{R}, a \in \mathcal{A}, p \in \{0, 1\}\}$, where $p = 1$ indicates the presence of attribute $a$ in region $r$, and $p = 0$ denotes its absence.

The goal is to develop a methodology that, given a free-text radiology report $T$ and the predefined sets of regions $\mathcal{R}$ and attributes $\mathcal{A}$, accurately extracts all region-attribute-presence labels. This methodology should accurately determine the presence or absence of each predefined disease or attribute in its corresponding anatomical Region of Interest (RoI) based on the free-text report $T$. Consequently, we can extract $\mathcal{Y}_i$ from each unstructured sample $(\mathbf{X}_i, T_i)$, enabling the training of vision models with $\mathbf{X}_i$ and its corresponding structured labels $\mathcal{Y}_i$.

### 2.2 In-Context Learning for Structured Report Extraction

In-context learning enables LLMs to extract structured region-attribute-presence labels from free-text radiology reports by leveraging task-specific instructions and contextual examples, eliminating the need for model fine-tuning.

The model is conditioned on the task instructions $\tau$, a target free-text report $T_t$, the predefined sets of anatomical regions $\mathcal{R}$ and attributes $\mathcal{A}$, and a set of solved examples $\mathcal{E} = \{(T_{\text{ex}_i}, \mathcal{Y}_{\text{ex}_i})\}$. Each example consists of a free-text report $T_{\text{ex}_i}$ and its corresponding structured report, denoted as $\mathcal{Y}_{\text{ex}_i} = \{(r_i, a_i, p_i) \mid r_i \in \mathcal{R}, a_i \in \mathcal{A}, p_i \in \{0, 1\}\}$.

Given these inputs, the language model $\mathcal{LM}$ maps them to the structured report $\mathcal{Y}_t$ for $T_t$:

$$\mathcal{LM}(\tau, \mathcal{E}, \mathcal{R}, \mathcal{A}, T_t) = \mathcal{Y}_t.$$

## 2.3 Causal Language Modeling for Structured Report Generation

We employ causal language modeling to fine-tune an LLM for structured report extraction from free-text radiology reports. The training data consists of task instructions $\tau$, predefined sets of anatomical regions $\mathcal{R}$ and attributes $\mathcal{A}$, a target free-text report $T$, and its corresponding structured report $\mathcal{Y} = \{(r_i, a_i, p_i) \mid r_i \in \mathcal{R}, a_i \in \mathcal{A}, p_i \in \{0,1\}\}$. These components are concatenated into a textual sequence for each instance in the dataset.

The goal of causal language modeling is to model the probability distribution over structured reports given the task description, predefined sets, and free-text report. This can be formulated as:

$$P(\mathcal{Y} \mid \tau, \mathcal{R}, \mathcal{A}, T).$$

The concatenated text sequences are tokenized, transforming each instance into a sequence of tokens. Let $U = \{u_1, u_2, \ldots, u_n\}$ denote the full tokenized sequence, where tokens are derived from: The task instructions: $u_{\tau_1}, u_{\tau_2}, \ldots, u_{\tau_N}$, the predefined anatomical regions: $u_{R_1}, u_{R_2}, \ldots, u_{R_M}$, the predefined attributes: $u_{A_1}, u_{A_2}, \ldots, u_{A_P}$, the free-text report: $u_{T_1}, u_{T_2}, \ldots, u_{T_Q}$, the structured report: $u_{y_1}, u_{y_2}, \ldots, u_{y_K}$. Using causal language modeling, the goal is to model the probability distribution over the structured report tokens given the preceding tokens. This can be rewritten in terms of tokenized sequences as follows:

$$P(u_{y_1}, u_{y_2}, \ldots, u_{y_K} \mid u_{\tau_1}, \ldots, u_{\tau_N}, u_{R_1}, \ldots, u_{R_M}, u_{A_1}, \ldots, u_{A_P}, u_{T_1}, \ldots, u_{T_Q})$$

where $u_{y_i}$ correspond to the tokens of the structured report, $u_{\tau_i}$ represent the task instruction tokens, $u_{R_i}$ encode the anatomical regions, $u_{A_i}$ represent the attributes and $u_{T_i}$ correspond to the free-text report. This formulation enables the model to generate structured reports in an autoregressive manner, where each token $u_{y_i}$ is predicted based on the preceding sequence.

## 3 Experiments and Results

The gold standard collection of the ImaGenome dataset, established through consensus by three radiologists, serves as the ground truth for evaluating all methods. A key advantage of this dataset is the availability of location identifiers for each disease finding. All examples used in ICL prompts were excluded from the evaluation set to ensure fair comparison. We report results for *Disease-Only* and *Location+Disease* extraction separately, with the latter covering all possible diseaseâŞlocation combinations and being a considerably more challenging task. Our review of the gold standard dataset also shows occasional oddities, such as a disease listed under a lung sub-region but not for the entire lung.

- **Disease labels:** 'lung opacity', 'pleural effusion', 'atelectasis', 'enlarged cardiac silhouette', 'pulmonary edema/hazy opacity', 'pneumothorax', 'consolidation', 'fluid overload/heart failure', 'pneumonia'.

- **Location identifiers:** 'right lung', 'right apical zone', 'right upper lung zone', 'right mid lung zone', 'right lower lung zone', 'right hilar structures', 'left lung', 'left apical zone', 'left upper lung zone', 'left mid lung zone', 'left lower lung zone', 'left hilar structures', 'right costophrenic angle', 'left costophrenic angle', 'mediastinum', 'upper mediastinum', 'cardiac silhouette', 'trachea'.

Note that all evaluation metrics are reported based on **affirmative** cases, since the goal is to detect disease presence rather than absence.

**In-Context Learning (ICL) Results:** Tables 1 and 2 show the performance of various open-weight models on *Disease-Only* and *Location+Disease* label extraction from reports respectively, using ICL. We report precision, recall, and F1-score. The model is given the task description, a target free-text radiology report, and 1, 2, 4, or 8 in-context example(s) to guide structured report generation.

**Table 1.** In-Context Learning (ICL) performance of open-weight General and Medical LLMs on *Disease-Only* structured report generation. (ICL@k: ICL with k examples)

| General LLMs | | | | | | | | | | | | |
|---|---|---|---|---|---|---|---|---|---|---|---|---|
| General LLM | ICL@1 | | | ICL@2 | | | ICL@4 | | | ICL@8 | | |
| | Prec. | Rec. | F1 | Prec. | Rec. | F1 | Prec. | Rec. | F1 | Prec. | Rec. | F1 |
| Qwen-2.5-0.5B | 49.1 | 20.8 | 29.3 | 38.6 | 18.0 | 24.5 | 40.5 | 18.7 | 25.6 | 33.1 | 13.2 | 18.9 |
| Qwen-2.5-1.5B | 50.3 | 39.2 | 44.1 | 57.1 | 45.7 | 50.8 | 55.5 | 51.7 | 53.5 | 34.1 | 13.9 | 19.7 |
| Qwen-2.5-3B | 56.7 | 41.3 | 47.8 | 56.4 | 51.8 | 54.0 | 49.9 | 45.2 | 47.5 | 54.0 | 58.6 | 56.2 |
| Qwen-2.5-7B | 89.6 | 56.3 | 69.1 | 93.5 | 59.6 | 72.8 | 84.9 | 54.7 | 66.5 | 75.4 | 63.1 | 68.7 |
| Qwen-2.5-14B | 91.1 | 68.0 | 77.9 | 90.8 | 76.5 | **83.0** | 91.0 | 62.6 | 74.2 | 83.0 | 74.1 | 78.3 |
| Qwen-2.5-32B | **93.6** | 69.5 | **79.7** | **92.0** | 73.9 | 82.0 | **92.7** | 70.3 | 79.9 | **93.5** | 69.1 | 79.5 |
| Qwen-2.5-72B | 85.0 | 74.2 | 79.2 | 87.1 | 76.7 | 81.6 | 91.5 | 71.5 | 80.3 | 86.2 | 75.5 | 80.5 |
| LlaMA-3.3-70B | 72.1 | **80.7** | 76.2 | 75.8 | **88.1** | 81.5 | 76.5 | **86.9** | **81.4** | 85.4 | **78.6** | **81.8** |
| DeepSeek-R1-70B | 85.0 | 60.8 | 70.9 | 79.6 | 80.1 | 79.9 | 85.7 | 70.5 | 77.3 | 78.6 | 57.0 | 66.1 |
| **Medical LLMs** | | | | | | | | | | | | |
| Medical LLM | ICL@1 | | | ICL@2 | | | ICL@4 | | | ICL@8 | | |
| | Prec. | Rec. | F1 | Prec. | Rec. | F1 | Prec. | Rec. | F1 | Prec. | Rec. | F1 |
| Meerkat-8B | 56.5 | 55.3 | 55.9 | 67.0 | 58.6 | 62.5 | 55.6 | 71.2 | 62.4 | N/A | N/A | N/A |
| Meerkat-70B | 77.9 | 64.2 | 70.4 | 76.9 | 75.6 | 76.2 | 76.6 | 80.3 | 78.4 | N/A | N/A | N/A |
| OpenBioLLM-8B | 35.9 | 82.5 | 50.1 | 46.0 | 86.1 | 60.0 | 38.2 | **91.1** | 53.8 | N/A | N/A | N/A |
| OpenBioLLM-70B | 79.0 | 74.8 | 76.8 | **78.8** | 74.9 | 76.8 | 74.3 | 84.3 | 79.0 | N/A | N/A | N/A |
| MedGemma-27B | **80.3** | **85.1** | **82.6** | 76.0 | **90.8** | **82.8** | **79.0** | **91.1** | **84.7** | **81.0** | **90.1** | **85.3** |

**Fine-Tuned Model Results:** Table 3 shows the performance of fine-tuned general-purpose and medical LLMs on the *Disease-Only* and *Location+Disease*

**Table 2.** In-Context Learning (ICL) performance of open-weight General and Medical LLMs on **Location+Disease** structured report generation. (ICL@k: ICL with k examples)

**General LLMs**

| General LLM | ICL@1 | | | ICL@2 | | | ICL@4 | | | ICL@8 | | |
|---|---|---|---|---|---|---|---|---|---|---|---|---|
| | Prec. | Rec. | F1 | Prec. | Rec. | F1 | Prec. | Rec. | F1 | Prec. | Rec. | F1 |
| Qwen-2.5-0.5B | 22.9 | 3.3 | 5.8 | 22.8 | 4.4 | 7.3 | 13.0 | 5.1 | 7.3 | 23.3 | 3.5 | 6.1 |
| Qwen-2.5-1.5B | 30.4 | 11.6 | 16.8 | 40.4 | 16.0 | 22.9 | 41.4 | 17.7 | 24.8 | 23.6 | 3.7 | 6.4 |
| Qwen-2.5-3B | 30.2 | 18.1 | 22.6 | 32.7 | 22.8 | 26.9 | 33.4 | 18.5 | 23.8 | 40.3 | 24.1 | 30.2 |
| Qwen-2.5-7B | 65.5 | 21.1 | 31.9 | 75.4 | 24.9 | 37.4 | 64.3 | 23.0 | 33.8 | 60.4 | 26.8 | 37.1 |
| Qwen-2.5-14B | 83.1 | 27.8 | 41.7 | 80.0 | 33.2 | 46.9 | **84.6** | 25.6 | 39.3 | 73.4 | 32.2 | 44.7 |
| Qwen-2.5-32B | **87.1** | 28.9 | 43.4 | **81.2** | 33.0 | 46.9 | 81.6 | 30.6 | 44.5 | 80.0 | 31.8 | 45.5 |
| Qwen-2.5-72B | 82.6 | 32.7 | 46.8 | 78.4 | 36.5 | 49.8 | 81.0 | 38.9 | 52.5 | 78.9 | 41.5 | 54.4 |
| LlaMA-3.3-70B | 69.5 | **37.7** | **48.9** | 68.8 | **50.5** | **58.2** | 71.6 | **46.8** | **56.6** | 80.6 | **44.9** | **57.6** |
| DeepSeek-R1-70B | 66.8 | 33.9 | 44.9 | 69.7 | 32.5 | 44.3 | 66.7 | 41.4 | 51.1 | 73.1 | 27.8 | 40.3 |

**Medical LLMs**

| Medical LLM | ICL@1 | | | ICL@2 | | | ICL@4 | | | ICL@8 | | |
|---|---|---|---|---|---|---|---|---|---|---|---|---|
| | Prec. | Rec. | F1 | Prec. | Rec. | F1 | Prec. | Rec. | F1 | Prec. | Rec. | F1 |
| Meerkat-8B | 60.5 | 27.9 | 38.2 | 63.9 | 25.6 | 36.5 | 45.4 | 41.4 | 43.3 | N/A | N/A | N/A |
| Meerkat-70B | 51.1 | 40.2 | 45.0 | 53.1 | 54.2 | 53.6 | 50.0 | 63.7 | 56.0 | N/A | N/A | N/A |
| OpenBioLLM-8B | 21.1 | **71.7** | 32.5 | 23.8 | 60.8 | 34.2 | 19.8 | **69.8** | 30.9 | N/A | N/A | N/A |
| OpenBioLLM-70B | **65.3** | 43.0 | 51.8 | **65.3** | 43.1 | 51.9 | 58.7 | 59.8 | 59.2 | N/A | N/A | N/A |
| MedGemma-27B | 65.3 | 57.0 | **60.9** | 62.4 | **64.3** | **63.3** | **61.9** | 69.1 | **65.3** | 63.4 | **70.5** | **66.8** |

tasks. The 72B Qwen model achieves the highest F1: 94.8% and 83.3% on the two tasks, respectively. The fine-tuned 8/70B Meerkat and 7B OpenBioLLM models often failed to produce the correct structured output format, which negatively affected their recall. This is likely due to their training data. Specifically, MedGemma was trained on diverse medical sources, including CXR radiology reports relevant to our task, whereas Meerkat was trained on chain-of-thought data from medical textbooks, which may contribute to its structural inconsistencies [7,10]. Also, due to their 8K context limits, Meerkat and OpenBioLLM cannot accommodate 8 in-context examples and are therefore marked as N/A.

### 3.1 Insights and Conclusions

**ICL vs. Fine-Tuning:** Fine-tuned models generally outperform ICL, with a 7B model matching the performance of a 72B ICL model across both tasks (Fig. 1).

**Table 3.** Performance of *Fine-tuned* General and Medical LLMs on the *Disease-Only* and *Location+Disease* structured report generation tasks.

| General LLMs | | | | | | |
|---|---|---|---|---|---|---|
| **Fine-tuned General LLM** | **Disease-Only** | | | **Location+Disease** | | |
| | Prec. | Rec. | F1 | Prec. | Rec. | F1 |
| Qwen-2.5-0.5B | 63.6 | 61.5 | 62.5 | 44.9 | 14.8 | 22.3 |
| Qwen-2.5-1.5B | 84.5 | 57.0 | 68.1 | 68.4 | 13.4 | 22.4 |
| Qwen-2.5-3B | 81.6 | 58.4 | 68.0 | 63.8 | 14.4 | 23.5 |
| Qwen-2.5-7B | 94.9 | 68.5 | 79.6 | 79.2 | 36.3 | 49.7 |
| Qwen-2.5-14B | 91.7 | 76.5 | 83.4 | 76.0 | 51.6 | 61.5 |
| Qwen-2.5-32B | 93.5 | 78.7 | 85.4 | 76.4 | 58.4 | 66.2 |
| Qwen-2.5-72B | **95.8** | **93.7** | **94.8** | **84.5** | **82.2** | **83.3** |
| Llama-3.3-70B | 88.4 | 92.6 | 90.5 | 74.5 | 81.2 | 77.7 |
| **Medical LLMs** | | | | | | |
| **Fine-Tuned Medical LLM** | **Disease-Only** | | | **Location+Disease** | | |
| | Prec. | Rec. | F1 | Prec. | Rec. | F1 |
| Meerkat-8B | 69.4 | 51.7 | 59.2 | 31.4 | 23.1 | 26.6 |
| Meerkat-70B | 82.0 | 58.2 | 68.1 | 53.0 | 23.7 | 32.7 |
| OpenBioLLM-8B | 89.6 | 74.2 | 81.2 | 68.1 | 28.9 | 40.6 |
| OpenBioLLM-70B | **95.2** | 87.5 | 91.2 | **78.5** | 71.4 | 74.8 |
| MedGemma-27B | 94.7 | **90.9** | **92.8** | 75.6 | **76.9** | **76.3** |

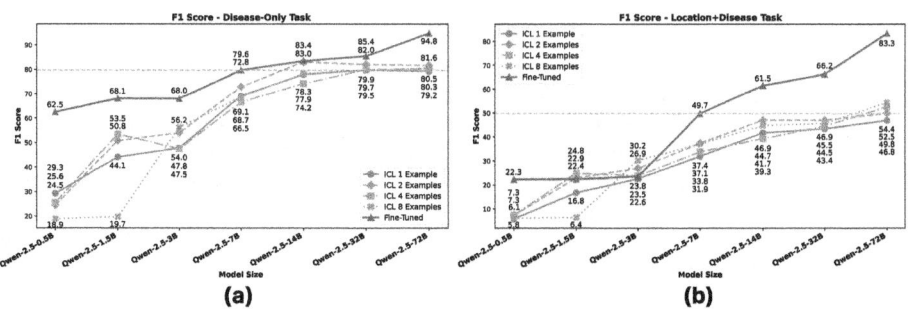

**Fig. 1.** F1 scores across Qwen models of different sizes for structured report generation. We compare fine-tuning with in-context learning (ICL) using varying numbers of examples. (a) shows results for Disease-Only, and (b) for Location+Disease. A fine-tuned 7B model matches the performance of a 72B ICL model across both tasks (gray dashed horizontal lines). (Color figure online)

Still, ICL has its strengths in low-resource settings. Smaller models like Qwen-2.5-1.5B and 3B, and medical LLMs like MedGemma and Meerkat, show better structure adherence under ICL (see Supplement for per-model adherence rates). For these models, fine-tuning led to more malformed outputs. Since we excluded those to isolate model knowledge, their reported metrics may be slightly inflated.

**Number of Examples:** Increasing ICL examples did not consistently boost performance. Most models saw marginal or negative gains from 2 to 4 and 4 to 8 examples. For Meerkat and OpenBioLLM, 8-shot inputs exceeded context limits. 2-shot inputs offered the best trade-off between performance and context length.

**Model Size:** Larger models generally outperformed smaller ones of the same architecture. While ICL underperforms fine-tuning overall, large ICL models (e.g., Qwen-2.5-32B/70B) can match the performance of smaller fine-tuned models (e.g., Qwen-2.5-7B), which may be useful when fine-tuning is infeasible.

**General vs. Medical LLMs:** MedGemma outperforms other medical models on both tasks and slightly surpasses the similarly sized Qwen-32B. In contrast, OpenBioLLM and Meerkat, which were trained on general biomedical or textbook-style data, perform worse than general LLMs of similar size. This suggests that medical LLMs trained on task-specific data have a clear advantage, especially for more difficult tasks like *Location+Disease* extraction.

**Conclusion:** Motivated by the evaluation gap in structured data extraction from free-text medical reports, we addressed it by extensively benchmarking open-weight general and medical LLMs on two structured data extraction tasks using both ICL and fine-tuning. Our results show that LLMs must be evaluated directly on structured extraction, not just downstream tasks. Under specific conditions, these models can produce highly accurate structured labels, with fine-tuning improving output consistency and compute efficiency.

# References

1. Bedi, S., et al.: Medhelm: holistic evaluation of large language models for medical tasks. arXiv preprint arXiv:2505.23802 (2025)
2. Busch, F., et al.: Large language models for structured reporting in radiology: past, present, and future. Eur. Radiol., 1–14 (2024)
3. Dehaghani, M.E., Sabour, A., Madu, A.B., Lourentzou, I., Moradi, M.: Representation learning with a transformer-based detection model for localized chest x-ray disease and progression detection. In: International Conference on Medical Image Computing and Computer-Assisted Intervention, pp. 578–587
4. Delbrouck, J.B., et al.: Automated structured radiology report generation. arXiv preprint arXiv:2505.24223 (2025)
5. Fink, M.A., et al.: Potential of ChatGPT and GPT-4 for data mining of free-text CT reports on lung cancer. Radiology **308**(3), e231362 (2023)
6. Gertz, R.J.: Potential of GPT-4 for detecting errors in radiology reports: implications for reporting accuracy. Radiology **311**(1), e232714 (2024)
7. Google: Medgemma hugging face (2025). https://huggingface.co/collections/google/medgemma-release-680aade845f90bec6a3f60c4 Accessed 04 June 2025

8. Irvin, J., et al.: CheXpert: a large chest radiograph dataset with uncertainty labels and expert comparison (2019)
9. Johnson, A.E., Pollard, T.J., Berkowitz, S.J., et al.: MIMIC-CXR, a de-identified publicly available database of chest radiographs with free-text reports. Sci. Data 1–8 (2019)
10. Kim, H., et al.: Small language models learn enhanced reasoning skills from medical textbooks. NPJ Digit. Med. **8**(1), 240 (2025). https://doi.org/10.1038/s41746-025-01653-8
11. Mallio, C.A., Sertorio, A.C., Bernetti, C., Beomonte Zobel, B.: Large language models for structured reporting in radiology: performance of GPT-4, ChatGPT-3.5, perplexity and bing. La radiologia medica **128**(7), 808–812 (2023)
12. Mbakwe, A.B., Wang, L., Moradi, M., Lourentzou, I.: Hierarchical vision transformers for disease progression detection in chest x-ray images. In: International Conference on Medical Image Computing and Computer-Assisted Intervention, pp. 685–695. Springer (2023)
13. Oakden-Rayner, L.: Exploring large-scale public medical image datasets. Acad. Radiol. **27**(1), 106–112 (2020). https://doi.org/10.1016/j.acra.2019.10.006 special Issue: Artificial Intelligence
14. Woźnicki, P., et al.: Automatic structuring of radiology reports with on-premise open-source large language models. Eur. Radiol. **35**(4), 2018–2029 (2025). https://doi.org/10.1007/s00330-024-11074-y
15. Wu, J.T., et al.: Chest ImaGenome dataset for clinical reasoning. In: Thirty-fifth Conference on Neural Information Processing Systems Datasets and Benchmarks Track (Round 2) (2021)

# NeuroReport-MS: Multi-scale Agentic AI for Automated Clinical Report Generation in Multiple Sclerosis

Khaoula Alaoui Belghiti[1]("), Nour Eddine Zekaoui[1], Mounia Mikram[1], and Maryem Rhanoui[2]

[1] School of Information Sciences, Rabat, Morocco
khaoula.alaouibelghiti@esi.ac.ma
[2] Laboratory Health Systemic Process (P2S), UR4129, University Claude Bernard Lyon 1, University of Lyon, Lyon, France

**Abstract.** Multiple Sclerosis (MS) is an incurable chronic autoimmune disease, heavily relies on comprehensive analysis of brain lesions from MRI scans for an accurate diagnosis and progression evaluation, a task that can be time-consuming and prone to inter-rater variability among neurologists. While existing computer-aided diagnosis (CAD) systems have made significant advances in lesion detection and segmentation, they still fail to bridge the gap between imaging findings and actionable insights. To address these limitations, we propose a novel agentic AI framework that unifies multi-scale feature extraction with interpretable reasoning. With a hierarchical attention network that integrates lesion-level, region-level, and global-level features to predict pathological involvement across 48 brain regions. Building upon this multi-scale foundation, a GPT-4o-based LLM agent orchestrates region classification and symptom mapping, dynamically querying a clinical knowledge database to generate patient-specific reports enabling advanced reasoning about lesion patterns and their clinical implications. Through comprehensive evaluation on 100 patients from public datasets, our framework outperforms SOTA architectures and achieves $0.85 \pm 0.04$ AUC in regional classification while delivering clinician-friendly interpretations. By converting imaging data into structured clinical insights, we advance AI based MS care from passive lesion quantification into active decision support; representing a paradigm shift toward agentic CAD systems.

**Keywords:** Multiple Sclerosis · Clinical Decision Support · Multi-Scale Analysis · Agentic AI · Large Language Models

## 1 Introduction

Multiple sclerosis (MS) is a chronic autoimmune disease affecting over 2.8 million people worldwide, where the immune system attacks the protective myelin shell covering nerve fibers, disrupting neural communication and leading to progressive disability. As an incurable condition with therapies primarily targeting symptom management, accurate MRI-based diagnosis and monitoring remain the cornerstone of clinical care and treatment planning. In addition the heterogeneous nature of MS lesions presents unique challenges for automated analysis; lesions exhibit considerable variability in size, shape, location, and signal characteristics across different imaging modalities. Moreover, their clinical significance depends not only on individual lesion characteristics but also on complex spatial relationships, regional distribution patterns, and cumulative brain burden. The current computer-aided diagnostic (CAD) systems for MS focus mainly on lesion detection and segmentation tasks, providing only binary masks or volumetric measurements [1]; therefore failing to translate imaging findings into actionable clinical insights that support decision-making. Recent advances in large language models (LLMs) and agentic AI systems present unprecedented opportunities to bridge this gap. By leveraging natural language processing capabilities and structured reasoning, these technologies can transform raw imaging data into interpretable clinical narratives. In this work, we propose NeuroReport-MS a comprehensive agentic framework for MS lesion analysis that addresses these limitations through intelligent orchestration of deep learning models and clinical knowledge bases. Our key contributions include: (1) a novel multi-scale feature extraction approach that combines lesion-level, region-level, and global contextual features within a hierarchical attention network for multi-label regional classification across 48 brain regions; (2) an agentic system that dynamically integrates clinical knowledge bases to map anatomical findings to expected neurological symptoms; and (3) automated generation of structured clinical reports using GPT-4o.

## 2 Related Work

Medical image analysis has achieved remarkable advances with deep learning models demonstrating unprecedented accuracy in detecting and segmenting anatomical structures [2]. In neurological disorders, this complexity has prompted multi-modal integration approaches [3] using deep learning to capture complex neuroimaging patterns [4]. Therefore, multi-scale analysis has emerged as a powerful paradigm for capturing biological systems' hierarchical nature. This approach effectively captures information at different levels; from fine anatomical details to global pathological patterns [2]. Feature pyramid networks [5] and attention mechanisms [6] have proven how models can leverage both local detail and global context successfully. However, multi-scale approaches within MS research remain surprisingly limited [7]. Existing implementations focus primarily on genomic-level data or disease progression trajectories [8], while most imaging-based methods operate at isolated scales: voxel-level for lesion segmentation [9], synthetic MRI generation [10], or global-level for disease classification [11], overlooking complex hierarchical relationships between individual lesions, anatomical regions, and whole-brain pathology. But still mostly focus on lesion detection and segmentation tasks [13], treating lesions as binary objects without considering their clinical significance; tracing a gap between what algorithms detect and what clinicians need for informed decisions. The integration of Large Language Models (LLMs) into healthcare has opened new possibilities for clinical decision support [12], with applications in medical question answering [14] and automated report generation. Yet LLM applications to MS diagnosis remain limited, focusing on analyzing progression from imaging reports using GPT models [15] or processing unstructured clinical documentation [16], operating primarily on text-based information rather than directly integrating structured imaging features with clinical reasoning. This landscape reveals a fundamental disconnect between technical findings and clinical insights. Our work addresses this gap by proposing the first agentic AI framework that combines multi-scale feature extraction with clinical reasoning capabilities.

## 3 Methodology

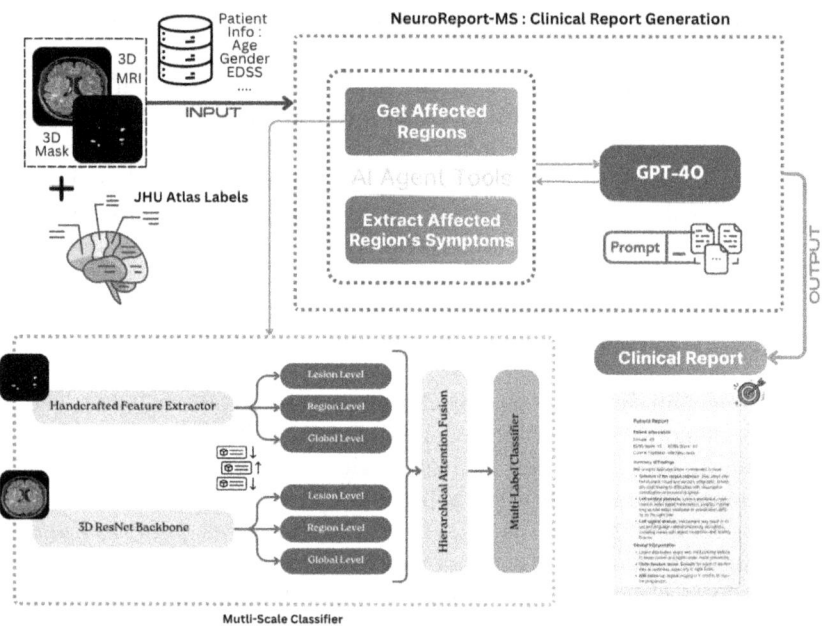

**Fig. 1.** NeuroReport-MS : an Agentic Clinical Report Generation Pipeline for Multiple Sclerosis.

NeuroReport-MS follows an agentic pipeline architecture consisting of three interconnected modules as displayed in Fig. 1: Multi-Scale Feature Extraction & Classification (bottom left), Knowledge Base Integration, and Clinical Report Generation using GPT-4o. The system takes as input patient information (age, gender, EDSS score, etc.), MRI scans with lesion masks, and leverages specialized tools for region classification and symptom mapping to produce comprehensive clinical reports.

**Multi-Scale Feature Extraction.** We designed a hierarchical attention model that learns from features extracted at three complementary scales, combining handcrafted insights with deep learning ones from a 3D ResNet backbone tailored for medical imaging, the model predicts lesion involvement across 48 white matter regions defined by the JHU atlas [18]; the primary sites of MS-related demyelination. The first extracts handcrafted features over 3 scales : **Scale 1: Lesion-Level Features**: identifying individual lesions from binarized lesion masks. including lesion volume, surface area, and intensity characteristics, reaching spatial features from distances to centroid and brain center. **Scale 2: Region-Level Features** : For each anatomical region defined by the JHU-ICBM atlas, we extracted : Regional lesion load and Number of lesions, spatial distribution as well as intensity characteristics of the region. **Scale 3: Global Features** represented by overall disease burden, spatial distribution patterns and connectivity disruption of the regions over the white matter. Together, these multi-scale features offer a rich and clinically relevant view of MS pathology, enhancing both model performance and interpretability.

**Attention Based Classifier.** Our model employs a 3D ResNet-inspired architecture for hierarchical feature extraction; Each ResNet block consists of 3D convolution with batch normalization, ReLU activation, 3D convolution with batch normalization, skip connection, and ReLU activation.

A 3D spatial attention module was integrated to focus on relevant regions:

$$\text{Attention}(X) = X \odot \sigma(f_{1\times1\times1}(\text{GAP}(X))) \tag{1}$$

where $\odot$ denotes element-wise multiplication, $\sigma$ is sigmoid activation, $f_{1\times1\times1}$ is a $1 \times 1 \times 1$ convolution, and global average pooling.

Followed by three-level feature extractors operating on the CNN backbone output; Lesion-Scale extractor; with global average pooling(1*1), Region-Scale extractor; with adaptive average pooling (2*2) and Global-Scale extractor; with adaptive average pooling (4*4). And all feature vectors are projected to 512 dimensions, and fused with hierarchical attention. Then we used a two-layer MLP for dimensionality reduction of the Handcrafted Features, so that the final classification layer combines CNN-derived and reduced features.

For the **Loss Function** We employed binary cross-entropy with logits loss for multi-label classification:

$$\mathcal{L} = -\frac{1}{N}\sum_{i=1}^{N}\sum_{j=1}^{C}[y_{ij}\log(\hat{y}_{ij}) + (1-y_{ij})\log(1-\hat{y}_{ij})] \tag{2}$$

where $N$ is batch size, $C$ is number of regions (48), $y_{ij}$ is ground truth, and $\hat{y}_{ij}$ is predicted probability.

**The Knowledge Base Integration.** follows an agentic architecture where the agent queries a vector database containing region-symptom mappings. The agent can access relevant clinical information based on the specific regions identified in the classification step, ensuring context-aware symptom mapping. The vector database stores structured mappings between anatomical regions and associated symptoms; representing direct functional consequences of lesions in those specific regions based on literature evidence.

**The Clinical Report Generation.** leverages the central GPT-4o LLM agent's natural language processing capabilities to synthesize information from multiple sources: Patient demographics and clinical history (age, gender, EDSS score, etc.), Regional classification results from the "Get Affected Regions" tool using the multi-label multi-scale classifier, Mapped symptoms from the "Extract Affected Regions Symptoms" tool quering the Vector database for comprehensive clinical knowledge Fig. 1.

The reports generated follow standardised clinical models and establish a clear correspondence between imaging results and symptoms, all instructed with a clear prompt identifying the GPT-4o as "clinical assistant specialized in Multiple Sclerosis (MS) diagnosis and medical report writing". They contain actionable information such as treatment follow-up recommendations and personalised follow-up suggestions. This ensures that results are both interpretable by clinicians and aligned with actual clinical workflows.

## 4 Experimental Setup

The network is implemented using PyTorch Framework for deep learning components, NiBabel and NiLearn for reading, manipulating, and visualizing MRI data, and scikit-learn for classical machine learning utilities, and trained on NVIDIA A100 Cloud GPUs. We use Adam optimizer with initial learning rate $\eta = 0.001$ and exponential decay, employed ReduceLROnPlateau with patience of 5 epochs, and Early stopping was implemented with validation loss plateau patience of 10 epochs.

**Dataset.** Our evaluation utilizes 100 patients from two public datasets: MSSEG-2 Challenge Dataset from MICCAI 2021: representing 3D FLAIR MRI MS scans and respective new lesion masks and The Consensus MS Dataset [17]: providing 3D MRI scans of 60 patients; each patient includes T1-weighted, T2-weighted, and FLAIR MRI sequences with corresponding manual lesion segmentations and patients meta information. The combined dataset encompasses various MS subtypes and disease stages, providing comprehensive evaluation coverage.

**Preprocessing and Registration.** All MRI scans were subjected to a standardized preprocessing, including skull stripping, intensity normalization, spatial registration to the MNI152 template space using affine transformation, and co-registration of lesion masks to corresponding MRI images. Plus standard 3D augmentations were applied during training including rotation, scaling and intensity variations.

**Evaluation Metrics :** We evaluate the system using multiple metrics: For classification performance: F1 score and AUC for each region, for the overall system performance opted for averaged metrics across all regions; For each brain region $j$, we computed: Precision, Recall, F1-score and AUC.

Report quality: we consulted clinical experts for the evaluation of some generated reports in terms of accuracy, clinical relevance, and actionable insights.

**Baseline Comparisons :** We compare our approach against three architectures : 3D nnUNet, Attention UNet; best performing models related to 3D medical imaging, and a standard ResNet classifier without the multi-scale integration (Table 1) :

Table 1. Model Performance Comparison

| Model | Params(M) | Loss | F1 Score | Macro AUC | Subset Acc |
|---|---|---|---|---|---|
| MultiScale-ResNet | 108.5 | **0.19** | **0.782** | **0.857** | **0.634** |
| Simple-3D-ResNet | 33.3 | 0.39 | 0.717 | 0.821 | 0.587 |
| 3D nnU-Net | 23.3 | 0.25 | 0.745 | 0.813 | 0.605 |
| 3D Attention-UNet | 95.8 | 0.23 | 0.758 | 0.839 | 0.612 |

## 5 Results and Discussion

**Regional Classification Performance.** Our multi-scale approach demonstrates superior performance across all evaluated regions. The hierarchical attention mechanism effectively combines information from different scales, achieving average AUC of 0.857; across all 48 regions, outperforming state-of-the-art deep learning models with minimum loss of 0.19 and an overall F1 score of 0.782. On a region level evaluation proved strongest performance in periventricular regions (AUC >0.90), with an F1 score of 0.94 on the "External capsule R"; capturing classic MS lesion patterns. While cortical areas also show solid detection (AUC 0.80–0.85) thanks to multi-scale analysis, deep gray matter remains more challenging (AUC 0.75–0.80) due to anatomical complexity. which reflects that regions with higher lesion frequency show better classification performance, while rare lesion locations benefit only from the global context features.

**Clinical Report Evaluation.** We presented some generated reports through our pipeline to neurology residents and radiologists, who reviewed the examples and found them to be highly reliable and useful in practice. About 92% accurately reflected the underlying imaging findings, while 88% captured all key clinical correlations to possible symptoms. Most reports were considered clear, well-structured, and easy to interpret, with 89% offered meaningful insights that could support real-world patient management decisions. These results demonstrate the potential for AI-driven systems to bridge the gap between imaging findings and clinical interpretation.

## 6 Conclusion

In this paper, we introduced NeuroReport-MS, a novel multi-scale agentic AI framework that transforms MS lesion analysis from passive detection to active clinical decision support. Our system demonstrates the potential of bridging advanced image processing with clinical reasoning, achieving strong classification performance ($0.85 \pm 0.04$ AUC) while generating clinically meaningful reports. The framework integrates three components: a multi-scale feature extraction network with hierarchical attention for multi-label classification across 48 brain regions, capturing lesion complexity with computational efficiency; a dynamic clinical knowledge base that contextualizes anatomical findings; and automated report generation using GPT-4o, delivering structured, actionable insights that support clinical decision-making. The system's strength lies particularly in leveraging anatomical structure and white matter atlas references to provide comprehensive regional analysis. While our results demonstrate promising clinical utility, several avenues for enhancement remain; where in future work will focus on longitudinal lesion tracking to capture disease progression patterns, validation on larger and more diverse patient datasets, and seamless integration into existing clinical workflows. Additionally, expanding the temporal scope of analysis and incorporating treatment response monitoring will further enhance the system's clinical impact. This work represents a significant step toward intelligent CAD systems that augment rather than replace clinical expertise.

**Acknowledgments.** We thank the MSSEG-2 challenge organizers for providing the dataset and the clinical experts who contributed to the knowledge base construction and report evaluation.

## References

1. Tahghighi, P., Zhang, Y., Souza, R., Komeili, A.: Enhancing new multiple sclerosis lesion segmentation via self-supervised pre-training and synthetic lesion integration. In: International Conference on Medical Image Computing and Computer-Assisted Intervention, pp. 263–272. Springer, Cham (2024)
2. Huo, X., et al.: HiFuse: hierarchical multi-scale feature fusion network for medical image classification. Biomed. Signal Process. Control **87**, 105534 (2024)
3. Praet, J., et al.: A future of AI-driven personalized care for people with multiple sclerosis. Front. Immunol. **15**, 1446748 (2024)
4. Haggag, R.M., Ali, E.M., Khalifa, M.E., Taha, M.: Multiple sclerosis diagnosis with brain MRI retrieval: a deep learning approach. Results Control Optim. **18**, 100533 (2025)
5. Alam, M.S., Wang, D., Sowmya, A.: AMFP-net: adaptive multi-scale feature pyramid network for diagnosis of pneumoconiosis from chest X-ray images. Artif. Intell. Med. **154**, 102917 (2024)
6. Chen, R., et al.: MedFuseNet: fusing local and global deep feature representations with hybrid attention mechanisms for medical image segmentation. Sci. Rep. **15**(1), 5093 (2025)

7. Kennedy, K.E., et al.: Multiscale networks in multiple sclerosis. PLoS Comput. Biol. **20**(2), e1010980 (2024)
8. Liu, C., et al.: Imageflownet: forecasting multiscale image-level trajectories of disease progression with irregularly-sampled longitudinal medical images. In: ICASSP 2025-2025 IEEE International Conference on Acoustics, Speech and Signal Processing (ICASSP), pp. 1–5. IEEE (2025)
9. Naeeni Davarani, M., et al.: Efficient segmentation of active and inactive plaques in FLAIR-images using DeepLabV3Plus SE with efficientnetb0 backbone in multiple sclerosis. Sci. Rep. **14**(1), 16304 (2024)
10. Belghiti, K.A., Rekik, I., Selim, S., Mounia, M., Rhanoui, M.: Spatial attention-enhanced diffusion model for multiple sclerosis MRI synthesis. In: Meets Africa Workshop, pp. 81–90. Springer Nature Switzerland, Cham (2024)
11. Amin, M., Nakamura, K., Ontaneda, D.: Differentiating multiple sclerosis from non-specific white matter changes using a convolutional neural network image classification model. Multiple Sclerosis Relat. Disord. **82**, 105420 (2024)
12. Ho, C.N., et al.: Qualitative metrics from the biomedical literature for evaluating large language models in clinical decision-making: a narrative review. BMC Med. Inform. Decis. Mak. **24**(1), 357 (2024)
13. Yousef, H., Malagurski Tortei, B., Castiglione, F.: Predicting multiple sclerosis disease progression and outcomes with machine learning and MRI-based biomarkers: a review. J. Neurol. **271**(10), 6543–6572 (2024)
14. Zekaoui, N.E., Mikram, M., Rhanoui, M., Yousfi, S.: BioMed-LLaMa-3: instruction-efficient fine-tuning of large language models for improved biomedical language understanding. In: International Conference on Multi-disciplinary Trends in Artificial Intelligence, pp. 399–410. Springer, Singapore (2024)
15. Joseph, A., Joseph, K., Joseph, A.: A pilot evaluation of the diagnostic accuracy of ChatGPT-3.5 for multiple sclerosis from case reports. Transl. Neurosci. **15**(1), 20220361 (2024)
16. Alnhwi, Z.A., et al.: Agreement of large language models with humans in extracting data from unstructured records of multiple sclerosis patients. Multiple Sclerosis Relat. Disord. **92**, 105969 (2024)
17. Muslim, A.M., et al.: Brain MRI dataset of multiple sclerosis with consensus manual lesion segmentation and patient meta information. Data Brief **42**, 108139 (2022)
18. JHU Atlas Labels. https://identifiers.org/neurovault.image:1408. Accessed 14 July 2025

# REMix: Refinement-Enhanced Visual-Textual Mixing for Lesion Segmentation

Soojin Hwang, Jaeyoon Sim, and Won Hwa Kim(✉)

Pohang University of Science and Technology (POSTECH), Pohang, South Korea
{soojin0622,simjy98,wonhwa}@postech.ac.kr

**Abstract.** Lesion segmentation is an essential task in medical imaging, aiding in the diagnosis and assessment of pulmonary diseases. While multi-modal approaches combining text with images improve segmentation by offering complementary cues, existing multi-modal models often utilize only a single abstract text source, and do not fully exploit its hierarchical interactions with visual features. In this work, we propose a novel multi-modal segmentation framework, i.e., REMix that refines and mixes image and text representations throughout the hierarchical decoding process. By adaptively structuring textual information and enhancing visual representations, our method effectively aligns both high-level semantics and fine-grained details. Extensive experiments on the QaTa-COV19 and MosMedData+ datasets demonstrate that our approach achieves superior segmentation performance, outperforming existing uni-modal and multi-modal methods.

**Keywords:** Vision-Language Modeling · Medical Image Segmentation

## 1 Introduction

Accurate segmentation in medical image analysis is essential task, aiding in the precise identification and diagnosis of various pathological conditions. Automated segmentation methods [8–14, 24] have been successful for assisting clinicians in detecting lesions and treatment. However, these models require large amounts of image data, which are often difficult to obtain due to privacy, cost, and demanding expert annotations. Moreover, relying solely on images lacks critical semantic details, such as the number and location of infected areas, which are typically described in medical reports by radiologists with clinically specialized terms, e.g., "unilateral" or "bilateral" [1].

To address these issues, recent studies leverage medical text prompts, which are naturally paired with medical images, eliminating the need for additional data acquisition process [2–4]. The text often offers complementary cues, serving as semantic guidance to compensate for quality deficiencies. However, these

---

S. Hwang and J. Sim—These authors contributed equally to this work.

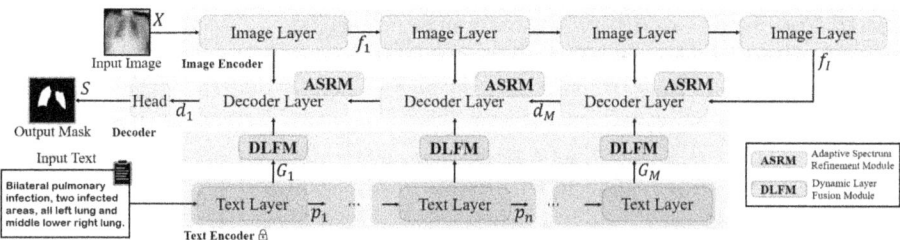

**Fig. 1. Architecture of REMix.** An input image $X$ and text prompt are fed into the image and text encoder, respectively. The text information $\hat{p}$ is refined through DLFM, while the image information $f$ is directly fed to the decoder, allowing visual features to be sequentially refined through ASRM to predict the output mask $S$.

models primarily focus on feature fusion rather than optimizing the them, and dependence on the final embedding of the text encoder neglects rich intermediate representations from earlier layers which lead to suboptimal performance.

In this paper, we propose **R**efinement-**E**nhanced Visual-Textual **Mix**ing Network (REMix), a novel multi-modal method for effective lesion segmentation by harnessing both image and text input at different context levels. To flexibly leverage hierarchical structure across text, we design Dynamic Layer Fusion Module (DLFM), which adaptively integrates full-range text features across decoding. Using this strategy, our approach enables the decoder to employ not only visual information but also comprehensive linguistic cues. For visual feature refinement, based on [5], we propose Adaptive Spectrum Refinement Module (ASRM) which captures global semantic content in the early stages and progressively incorporate local details. ASRM dynamically adjusts the kernel bandwidth to refine features at different decoding stages to boost relevant visual cues at each phase. Finally, integrating refined image and text features via attention mechanisms produces a harmonized decoder, leading to more accurate lesion segmentation.

In summary, REMix offers the following **key contributions: 1)** REMix refines image and text inputs by dynamically acquiring desirable features from both modalities for medical image segmentation. **2)** REMix shows superior performance on lesion segmentation compared to the state-of-the-art methods. **3)** Extensive validation was performed on two independent lung infection benchmarks, QaTa-COV19 and MosMedData+ datasets, to assess the effectiveness and generalizability of our model.

## 2 Method

Our goal is to generate a pixel-wise mask of infected lung regions from the image-text pair. To achieve this, our method consists of 3 main components including an image encoder, a text encoder, and a mask decoder, as shown in Fig. 1.

**Image and Text Encoder.** Given an image $X \in \mathbb{R}^{H \times W \times 3}$, we extract multiple image features $\{f_i\}_{i=1}^{I}$ where $f_i \in \mathbb{R}^{\frac{H}{2^{i+1}} \times \frac{W}{2^{i+1}} \times C_i}$ using ConvNeXt-Tiny [18] as an image encoder. Here, $H$ and $W$ denote the height and width of $X$, and $C_i$ is the feature dimensions at the $i$-th layer. For an input text, we adopt the pre-trained CXR-BERT [19] as a text encoder and extract a sequence of hidden features $\{P_n\}_{n=1}^{N}$ from $N$ layers with the text embedding $p_i \in \mathbb{R}^{L \times C_P}$ with length of $L$ in dimension of $C_P$. These features encode different levels of information from the input text, with higher indices representing high-level information.

To better align with the structure of a decoder and exploit the hierarchical text embeddings, we introduce a Dynamic Layer Fusion Module (DLFM) which constructs the representative textual embedding of each group based on semantic levels. We split the hidden features $P$ into $M$ groups, denoted as $G_m = \{p_j | j \in [\lceil \frac{N}{M} \cdot (m-1) + 1 \rceil, \lceil \frac{N}{M} \cdot m \rceil]\}$ for $1 \leq m \leq M$, where $M$ is the number of decoder layers. Then, $G_M$ is fed into the first decoder layer, while $G_{M-1}$ to $G_1$ are sequentially passed to the following layers. For each $G_m$, REMix dynamically learn the contribution $w_j$ of the $j$-th hierarchical text embedding within the $m$-th group, parameterized by $\alpha_m$ as $w_j = \frac{e^{\alpha_j}}{\sum_{j \in G_m} e^{\alpha_j}}$. Finally, the refined text embedding $t_m \in \mathbb{R}^{L \times C_H}$ at each decoder stage is computed as

$$t_m = \sum_{i=s_m}^{e_m} w_i \cdot p_i \tag{1}$$

at the $m$-th group of the text encoder, which fed into the corresponding decoder layer, enabling effective use of textual information across multiple levels.

**Mask Decoder.** As shown in Fig. 2, to obtain the feature $d_m$ from the $m$-th decoder, i.e., a feature that mixes both text and image characteristics, the $i$-th image embedding $f_i$, the $m$-th refined text embedding $t_m$, and the $(m+1)$-th decoder output $d_{m+1}$ are required, where the decoder input feature of $M$-th decoder $d_{M+1}$ is replaced by $f_I$. Before integration, we align text and image token dimensions by projecting $t_m$ to $\hat{t}_m \in \mathbb{R}^{L' \times C_i}$ using a transformation defined as $\hat{t}_m = \text{ReLU}(\text{Conv}(t_m W_t))$. Here, $L'$ represents the number of tokens after projection, $W_t$ is a learnable parameter, and $\text{Conv}(\cdot)$ denotes a $1 \times 1$ convolutional layer. The obtained $\hat{t}_m$ will be matched with the visual feature later.

To refine the visual feature, we propose Adaptive Spectrum Refinement Module (ASRM) that enhances either coarse semantic information or fine-grained details adaptively at each decoder stage, ensuring balanced multi-level representations. As proposed in [5], the refined visual feature $\hat{d}_m$ of the $m$-th decoder layer is obtained from $d_m$ as

$$\hat{d}_m = \text{IFFT}(\text{FFT}(d_m) \odot g_{m,\sigma_m}) + d_m \tag{2}$$

where $\odot$ is element-wise multiplication, $g_{m,\sigma_m}$ is a Gaussian filtering coefficient map with kernel bandwidth $\sigma_m$, matching $d_m$'s spatial dimensions and FFT and IFFT represent Fourier Transform and Inverse Fourier Transform, respectively. Here, $\sigma_m$ is learnable, flexibly capturing of local-to-global visual properties.

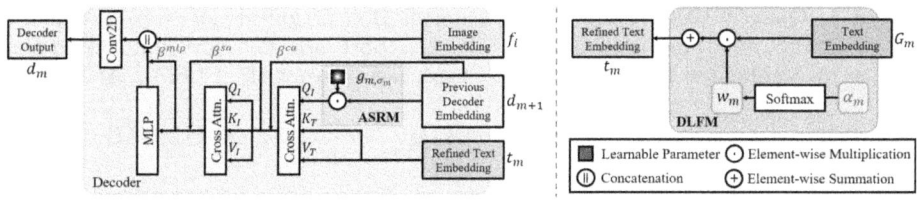

**Fig. 2. Illustration of key modules in REMix.** Left: Decoder with adaptive spectrum refinement module (ASRM). Right: Dynamic layer fusion module (DLFM).

With refined visual feature $\hat{d}_m$ and textual embedding $\hat{t}_m$, the multi-head cross-attention (MHCA) mechanism [21] fuses textual guidance with visual information, producing a text-guided visual representation as

$$d_m^{ca} = \hat{d}_m + \beta^{ca}(\text{LN}(\text{MHCA}(\hat{d}_m, \hat{t}_m))) \quad (3)$$

where $\text{LN}(\cdot)$ is layer normalization [20], and $\beta^{ca}$ is a trainable parameter controlling the weight of the residual connection. Next, the obtained representation $d_m^{ca}$ is inputted to a multi-head self-attention (MHSA) operation to enhance contextual relationships within the decoder embedding itself as

$$d_m^{sa} = d_m^{ca} + \beta^{sa}(\text{LN}(\text{MHSA}(d_m^{ca}))) \quad (4)$$

where $\beta^{sa}$ is also a learnable parameter. Then, the enhanced visual representation $d_m^{sa}$ is then passed to a Multi-Layer Perceptron (MLP) with an activation and residual connection, and produce a final visual feature as

$$d_m = d_m^{sa} + \beta^{mlp}(\text{MLP}(d_m^{sa})) \quad (5)$$

where $\beta^{mlp}$ is a learnable weight that adjusts the residual connection.

Afterwards, the mixed multi-modal feature $d_m \in \mathbb{R}^{(H \times W) \times C_m}$ is reshaped and upsampled to derive $d_m^u \in \mathbb{R}^{H' \times W' \times C_m}$, which is denoted as

$$d_m^u = \text{Upsample}(\text{Reshape}(d_m)). \quad (6)$$

To compute the final decoder output $d_m^o \in \mathbb{R}^{H' \times W' \times C_{m-1}}$, the $d_m^u$ is concatenated with $f_m \in \mathbb{R}^{H' \times W' \times C_m}$ on the channel dimension, where $f_m$ is the low-level features obtained from visual encoder via skip connection, derived as

$$d_m^o = \text{ReLU}(\text{Conv}([d_m^u, f_m])) \quad (7)$$

where $[\cdot, \cdot]$ represents the concatenate operation on the channel dimension. Finally, the final output $S$ is derived from the final decoder feature map $d_1^o$ as $S = \text{Sigmoid}(\text{Conv}(\text{Upsample}(d_1^o)))$, which produces pixel-wise segmentation.

**Table 1.** Quantitative comparison on segmentation of uni-modal (top) and multi-modal (middle) learning baselines, and REMix (bottom). The best and second-best results are highlighted in **bold** and underlined, respectively. (D: DLFM / A: ASRM)

| Method | Type | Param ↓ (M) | FLOPs ↓ (G) | QaTa-COV19 DSC ↑ | IoU ↑ | MosMedData+ DSC ↑ | IoU ↑ |
|---|---|---|---|---|---|---|---|
| UNet [8] | CNN | **14.8** | 50.3 | 79.02 | 69.46 | 64.60 | 50.73 |
| UNet++ [9] | CNN | 74.5 | 94.6 | 79.62 | 70.25 | 71.75 | 58.39 |
| nnUNet [10] | CNN | <u>19.1</u> | 412.7 | 80.42 | 70.81 | 72.59 | 60.36 |
| TransUNet [12] | Hybrid | 105 | 56.7 | 78.63 | 69.13 | 71.24 | 58.44 |
| Swin-UNet [13] | Hybrid | 82.3 | 67.3 | 78.07 | 68.34 | 63.29 | 50.19 |
| CLIP [15] | Hybrid | 87.0 | 105.3 | 79.81 | 70.66 | 71.97 | 59.64 |
| LAVT [17] | Hybrid | 118.6 | 83.8 | 79.28 | 69.89 | 73.29 | 60.41 |
| LViT [2] | Hybrid | 29.7 | 54.1 | 83.66 | 75.11 | 74.57 | 61.33 |
| GuideDecoder [3] | Hybrid | 44.0 | <u>22.4</u> | 89.78 | 81.45 | 77.75 | 63.60 |
| MMI-UNet [4] | Hybrid | 56.2 | **22.1** | <u>90.88</u> | <u>83.28</u> | <u>78.42</u> | <u>64.50</u> |
| REMix (w/o D+A) | Hybrid | 44.7 | 22.5 | 91.06 | 83.58 | 78.28 | 64.31 |
| REMix (w/o D) | Hybrid | | | 91.10 | 83.66 | 78.90 | 65.16 |
| REMix (w/o A) | Hybrid | | | 91.13 | 83.71 | 78.70 | 64.88 |
| REMix (Ours) | Hybrid | | | **91.17** | **83.78** | **79.44** | **65.90** |

## 3 Experiments

### 3.1 Datasets and Experimental Settings

**Datasets.** We followed the setup provided in [2] and [4]. Two datasets, i.e., Qata-COV19 (QATA) [6] and MosMedData+ (MOSMED) [7], were used in our experiments to evaluate the performance of REMix. The QATA dataset, compiled by researchers from Qatar University and Tampere University, includes 9258 COVID-19 chest X-ray images, which was partitioned into training, validation, and testing sets, with 5716, 1429, and 2113 samples, respectively. Similarly, the MOSMED dataset consists of 2729 CT scan slices of lung infections, partitioned into 2183 for training, 273 for validation, and 273 for testing. Both datasets provide similar clinical factors as text annotations such as infection in lungs, lesion count, and approximate location of the infected areas.

**Experimental Settings.** We designed medical image segmentation experiments to detect infected lung areas from image-text pairs. For quantitative evaluation, we employed the Dice coefficient (DSC) and IoU metrics to measure overlap between predicted and ground truth masks, as done in [2]. For optimization, we employed a combination of Dice loss and Cross-Entropy loss using the AdamW [22] optimizer with a batch size of 32. The learning rate follows a cosine annealing schedule, starting at 3e-4 and decreasing to 1e-6. Training and testing were performed on a single NVIDIA RTX A6000 GPU with 48GB of memory.

## 3.2 Performance Comparison with SOTA Methods

**Quantitative Results.** Table 1 reports the results of REMix and recent unimodal and multi-modal baselines, where the baseline results are adopted from [4]. REMix surpassed all baselines on QATA and MOSMED, improving DSC by 10.75% and 6.85% over the best uni-modal approach. It highlights the efficacy of incorporating text features in improving segmentation results. When compared to multi-modal methods [3] and [4], REMix achieves DSC gains of 1.19% and 0.29% on QATA, and 1.69% and 1.02% on MOSMED.

Assessing the key modules, i.e., DLFM and ASRM, DSC and IoU increased by 1.16% and 1.59% on MOSMED, respectively when included, proving the effectiveness of semantic information jointly embedded in both text and images. Furthermore, while previous SOTA model requires 56.2M parameters [4], REMix performs better with only 44.7M with DLFM and ASRM.

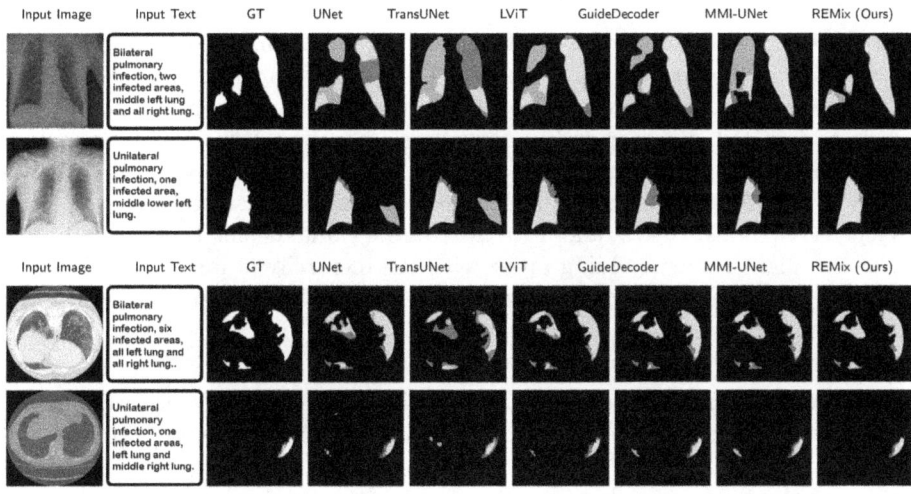

**Fig. 3.** Visualization of segmentation results. Top: Results on QaTa-COV19 dataset, Bottom: results on MosMedData+ dataset. Yellow, red, and green represent true positive, false negative, and false positive, respectively. (Color figure online)

**Qualitative Results.** Figure 3 shows qualitative comparisons of REMix with five baselines (i.e., two uni-modal, three multi-modal) on QATA and MOSMED. Overall, REMix demonstrates superior segmentation performance in two key aspects. First, REMix effectively captures challenging pixels missed by baselines.

For instance, in the second row of Fig. 3 (top), uni-modal works identified unnecessary regions, while REMix accurately segmented the infection, benefiting from the textual guidance such as "one infected area". Second, REMix notably reduces false-positives. As shown in the first row of Fig. 3 (top) and the second row of Fig. 3 (bottom), other methods tend to over-segment the infected areas, whereas REMix accurately produce more precise and compact masks. This highlights its robustness in handling fine-grained details and difficult regions.

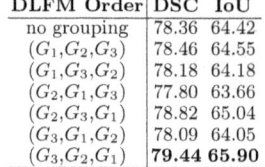
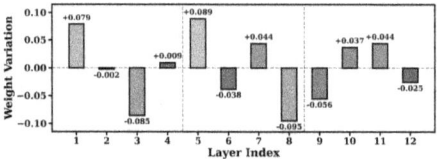
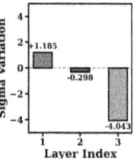

| DLFM Order | DSC | IoU |
|---|---|---|
| no grouping | 78.36 | 64.42 |
| $(G_1,G_2,G_3)$ | 78.46 | 64.55 |
| $(G_1,G_3,G_2)$ | 78.18 | 64.18 |
| $(G_2,G_1,G_3)$ | 77.80 | 63.66 |
| $(G_2,G_3,G_1)$ | 78.82 | 65.04 |
| $(G_3,G_1,G_2)$ | 78.09 | 64.05 |
| $(G_3,G_2,G_1)$ | **79.44** | **65.90** |

**Fig. 4.** Left: Case study on the impact of grouping order on the MOSMED dataset. Center: Variation of $w$ values across text embedding layers for $(G_3, G_2, G_1)$. Right: Variation of $\sigma$ values across decoder layers.

**Effect of Embedding Order in Text Representations.** To validate DLFM, we examined the effect of text embedding order on segmentation. In the Fig. 4 (left), we grouped text embeddings into three sets corresponding to decoder layers and tested different group sequences. The first row, where the entire text embeddings are given to each decoder layer with equal weights, achieves reasonable performance, but our hierarchical grouping strategy, particularly $(G_3, G_2, G_1)$, boosts DSC and IoU up to 79.44 and 65.90, respectively. This structure aligns the embedding order with the hierarchy of image encoder, suggesting that incorporating high-level semantics early and fine-grained details later is more effective.

**Analyzing Parameter Learning per Module.** In Fig. 4(center), we explored the changes in text embedding contributions after training by uniformly initializing before optimization. Contrary to prior assumptions [3,4], the embedding weight of the final layer decreases by 0.025, showing that relying solely on it does not improve segmentation. Instead, adaptively distributing weight across all embeddings enhances performance, emphasizing the role of ordering in medical text-driven segmentation. The Fig. 4 (right) shows how the $\sigma$ in ASRM change across decoders. Early decoders emphasize global features with larger $\sigma$, while later decoders reduce it by 4.043 to focus on details. This indicates that our modules refine the visual representation through successive decoders.

## 4 Conclusion

In this work, we proposed REMix, a multi-modal segmentation framework that progressively refines image and text representations and integrates them across the sequential decoding process. REMix dynamically extracts and refines commonly important information from both modalities to ensure a hierarchical integration of high-level semantics and fine-grained details. Experiments on QaTa-COV19 and MosMedData+ show that REMix outperforms state-of-the-art models, which validates the advantage of structured multi-modal refinement. REMix further demonstrates strong adaptability to diverse textual formats, showcasing its potential for practical applicability to real-scenarios.

**Acknowledgements.** This research was supported by RS-2024-00437866(50%), RS-2022-II2202290 (40%), and RS-2019-II191906 (AI Graduate Program at POSTECH, 10%).

# References

1. Larson, D.B., Towbin, A.J., Pryor, R.M., et al.: Improving consistency in radiology reporting through the use of department-wide standardized structured reporting. Radiology **267**(1) (2013)
2. Li, Z., et al.: LVIT: language meets vision transformer in medical image segmentation. IEEE Trans. Med. Imaging **43**(1) (2023)
3. Zhong, Y., et al.: Ariadne's thread: using text prompts to improve segmentation of infected areas from chest x-ray images. In: International Conference on Medical Image Computing and Computer-Assisted Intervention (2023)
4. Bui, P.N., Le, D.T., Choo, H.: Visual-textual matching attention for lesion segmentation in chest images. In: International Conference on Medical Image Computing and Computer-Assisted Intervention (2024)
5. Liu, Y., Bai, S., Li, G., et al.: Open-vocabulary segmentation with semantic-assisted calibration. In: Proceedings of the IEEE/CVF Conference on Computer Vision and Pattern Recognition (2024)
6. Degerli, A., Kiranyaz, S., et al.: Osegnet: operational segmentation network for Covid-19 detection using chest x-ray images. In: 2022 IEEE International Conference on Image Processing (ICIP). IEEE (2022)
7. Morozov, S.P., Andreychenko, A.E., Pavlov, N.A., et al.: Mosmeddata: chest CT scans with COVID-19 related findings dataset. arXiv preprint arXiv:2005.06465 (2020)
8. Ronneberger, O., Fischer, P., Brox, T.: U-net: convolutional networks for biomedical image segmentation. In: Medical Image Computing and Computer-Assisted Intervention–MICCAI (2015)
9. Zhou, Z., Siddiquee, R., Mahfuzur, M., Tajbakhsh, N., et al.: Unet++: a nested u-net architecture for medical image segmentation. In: Deep Learning in Medical Image Analysis and Multimodal Learning for Clinical Decision Support: 4th International Workshop, DLMIA 2018, and 8th International Workshop, ML-CDS 2018, Held in Conjunction with MICCAI 2018
10. Isensee, F., et al.: nnU-Net: a self-configuring method for deep learning-based biomedical image segmentation. Nature Methods **18**(2) (2021)
11. Hatamizadeh, A., Tang, Y., Nath, V., et al.: Unetr: transformers for 3D medical image segmentation. In: Proceedings of the IEEE/CVF Winter Conference on Applications of Computer Vision (2022)

12. Chen, Ji., Lu, Y., et al.: Transunet: transformers make strong encoders for medical image segmentation. Med. Image Anal. (2024)
13. Cao, H., Wang, Y, et al.: Swin-unet: Unet-like pure transformer for medical image segmentation. In: European Conference on Computer Vision (2022)
14. Hatamizadeh, A., Nath, V., et al.: Swin unetr: swin transformers for semantic segmentation of brain tumors in MRI images. In: International MICCAI Brainlesion Workshop (2021)
15. Radford, A., Kim, J.W., Hallacy, C., et al.: Learning transferable visual models from natural language supervision. In: International Conference on Machine Learning, PMLR (2021)
16. Kim, W., Son, B., Kim, I.: Vilt: Vision-and-language transformer without convolution or region supervision. In: International Conference on Machine Learning, PMLR (2021)
17. Yang, Z., Wang, J., Tang, Y., et al.: LAVT: language-aware vision transformer for referring image segmentation. In: Proceedings of the IEEE/CVF Conference on Computer Vision and Pattern Recognition (2022)
18. Liu, Z., Mao, H., et al.: A convnet for the 2020s. In: Proceedings of the IEEE/CVF Conference on Computer Vision and Pattern Recognition (2022)
19. Boecking, B., Usuyama, N., Bannur, S., Castro, Daniel C., et al.: Making the most of text semantics to improve biomedical vision–language processing. In: European Conference on Computer Vision (2022)
20. Ba, J.L., Kiros, J.R., Hinton, G.E.: Layer normalization. IN: NIPS (2016)
21. Vaswani, A., Shazeer, N., Parmar, N., et al.: Attention is all you need. In: Advances in Neural Information Processing Systems, vol. 30 (2017)
22. Loshchilov, I., Hutter, F.: Decoupled weight decay regularization. In: International Conference on Learning Representations (2017)
23. LNCS Homepage. http://www.springer.com/lncs. Accessed 25 May 2023
24. Cho, H., Han, Y., Kim, W.H.: Anti-adversarial consistency regularization for data augmentation: applications to robust medical image segmentation. In: International Conference on Medical Image Computing and Computer-Assisted Intervention (2023)
25. Liew, Y.Z., et al.: 3D medical image segmentation via sequential 2D slice processing. ICT Express (2025)
26. Shamshiri, S., Sohn, I.: Security methods for AI based COVID-19 analysis system: a survey. ICT Express **8**(4) (2022)

# An LLM-Based Active Assistant and Smart Manual for CT Imaging Workflows

Zeinab Aliakbari Mamaghani[1(✉)], Linda Vorberg[1,2], Andreas Maier[1], Alexander Katzmann[2], and Oliver Taubmann[2]

[1] Friedrich-Alexander University Erlangen-Nuremberg, Erlangen, Germany
{zeinab.aliakbari,linda.vorberg,andreas.maier}@fau.de
[2] Computed Tomography, Siemens Healthineers, Forchheim, Germany
{alexander.katzmann,oliver.taubmann}@siemens-healthineers.com

**Abstract.** Performing medical imaging exams ideally requires technologists to have deep clinical knowledge and technical expertise to operate scanners effectively and efficiently. However, there is a shortage of highly qualified workforce in radiology while patient volumes are rising steadily. Therefore, intelligent assistance is needed to streamline workflow adjustments and reduce manual workload. This study presents a Large Language Model (LLM)-based chatbot to assist clinical staff in Computed Tomography (CT) protocol and postprocessing setup by integrating device-specific information and patient-specific clinical data. As an active assistant integrated in a scan workflow prototype, it provides responses with actionable links that allow users to modify protocol settings directly. At the same time, it acts as a smart manual enhanced with patient-specific context, referencing and linking to both official device documentation as well as clinical indication and prior diagnostic reports. This is realized with an advanced Retrieval Augmented Generation (RAG) with pre- and post-retrieval strategies to improve contextual relevance. An LLM-based evaluation was employed to assess performance. We achieved 95.0% alignment with predefined expectations using GPT-4o mini, and 98.3% with GPT-4o. To evaluate the effect of the applied techniques, an ablation study was conducted. Omitting few-shot examples and instruction-based prompting reduced expectation alignment to 71.4% and 60.5%, respectively. When both were removed, it decreased to 55.0%. The findings underscore the effectiveness of prompt engineering in guiding LLMs to produce accurate, clinically relevant outputs in the correct format.

**Keywords:** CT workflow assistant · LLM · Prompt engineering techniques

---

A. Katzmann and O. Taubmann—These authors contributed equally to this work.

---

**Supplementary Information** The online version contains supplementary material available at https://doi.org/10.1007/978-3-032-07502-4_6.

## 1 Introduction

Choosing ideal CT acquisition parameters, creating relevant reconstructions, and obtaining adequate post-processing results requires deep technical knowledge of the scanner, as well as careful consideration of patient-specific conditions and clinical indications. Due to the limited availability of skilled radiology staff and the increasing demand for imaging, this becomes a challenge. Therefore, reducing manual workload and streamlining protocol adjustment through intelligent decision support has the potential to enhance accuracy, improve workflow efficiency, and increase patient care quality.

Several studies have explored the use of machine learning and natural language processing (NLP) techniques to support decision-making in CT and Magnetic Resonance Imaging (MRI) protocol assignment [1–3]. Building upon these foundations, recent research has begun to explore the potential of LLMs in radiology workflows [4]. A relevant study [5] compared ChatGPT's responses to the American College of Radiology (ACR) Appropriateness Criteria (AC) for breast pain and cancer screening, assessing its ability to provide appropriate imaging procedures and modalities for clinical workflow improvement. Another study [6] investigated the potential of an AI-driven chatbot to offer personalized imaging recommendations by developing a context-aware system using ChatGPT-3.5-turbo and the ACR AC documents as its specialized knowledge base. Similarly, Gertz et al. [7] explored GPT-4's ability to determine the most appropriate imaging strategy based on patients' medical histories and clinical questions derived from the Radiology Resident Forum (RRF). However, using an LLM alone is not sufficient to ensure clinically accurate answers. One key limitation is the phenomenon of hallucination, where the model generates outputs that are factually incorrect or unsupported by real data [8,9]. Furthermore, Gertz et al. [7] highlighted concerns about transparency, as the specific guidelines and references behind LLM-generated recommendations are often unclear, making it difficult to ensure accountability in clinical decision-making.

The primary objective of this study is to develop a chatbot that serves as an intelligent assistant for CT workflow adjustment by providing accurate, context-aware responses with actionable hyperlinks to relevant CT acquisition and post-processing settings. By leveraging an advanced RAG architecture [10] that integrates device-specific information and patient clinical data, we mitigate hallucination. This study distinguishes itself by integrating the technical capabilities of scanners, whereas prior work primarily focused on patient clinical conditions and assumed staff familiarity with device functionalities. By addressing the limited practical knowledge of staff regarding diverse new-generation scanners, our approach provides more context-aware recommendations for customizing protocol settings. We employed multiple prompting techniques [11] to guide the LLM in generating responses enriched with actionable markup and providing references for its suggestions linked to relevant information in device documentation, clinical indications, or prior radiology reports. Furthermore, we introduce an LLM-based evaluation method to assess the chatbot's responses. This approach is adaptable and applicable to other domains where comprehensive human evaluation is not feasible.

## 2 Methodology

The architecture of the chatbot system is illustrated in the diagram shown in Fig. 1. The chatbot serves as a component within an application designed to adjust CT scan protocols for patients. The implementation of the chatbot framework is described in detail below.

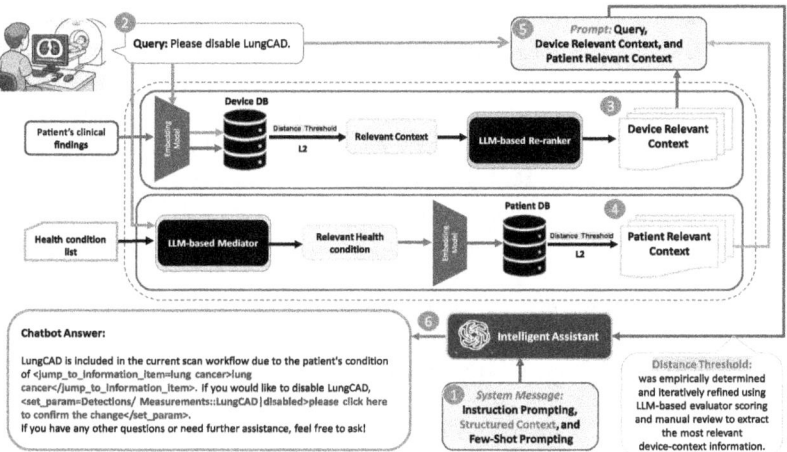

**Fig. 1.** Overview of chatbot operation: First, (1) we set the system message with a model role prompt and output formatting guidelines. After receiving the user query (2), the device (3) and patient context retrieval pipelines (4) are triggered, which are incorporated into the augmented prompt (5) and delivered to the LLM, which generates the final answer (6).

### 2.1 Data Sources

The foundation of the chatbot's RAG architecture relies on two vector databases: first, a device vector database, created from scanner documentation, in our exemplary scenario the official device manuals of a Naeotom Alpha CT scanner (Siemens Healthineers AG, Forchheim, Germany). When a new document is added, a function triggers a pipeline to clean, chunk, vectorize, and store it in the device vector database; and second, a patient vector database, dynamically generated from unstructured patient clinical reports. While these reports were uploaded by the user at the beginning of the chat session in our standalone prototype, they may be fetched automatically in an integrated system. OpenAI's *text-embedding-3-small* embedding model is used to transform content into vectors. In addition to these databases, a module within the host application processes the patient clinical reports to extract relevant information, such as clinical findings, indications, and the standard base protocol for the patient. This information is then used as *structured context* for the chatbot's operation.

## 2.2 Operational Workflow

At the beginning of each chat session, a **System Message** is created and sent to the LLM. As depicted in (1) in Fig. 1, it contains role assignment, task definition, tags specification and their usage, structured context, instruction-based prompting, and few-shot prompting. The instruction-based prompting is combined with emotion prompting [12] to guide the LLM on how to utilize the context, which tags to apply, and where they should appear in the answers. Further, we incorporate few-shot prompting, providing 10 question-answer examples, and the Chain-of-Thought (CoT) [11] technique to guide the LLM to use tags in its responses in the correct format.

Upon receiving a query (2), two context retrieval pipelines (3, 4) are triggered to extract relevant context from the device and patient databases. As depicted in (3), the **Device Context Retrieval Pipeline** begins with a vector similarity search. The embedding model converts the user's query into a vector. This query vector, along with a vector representing the patient's clinical findings, are both compared against the device vector database using Euclidean (L2) distance to retrieve up to 20 potentially relevant chunks.

To improve contextual relevance, a distance threshold is applied to filter extracted contexts, which was chosen empirically. Even after applying the threshold, we rarely observed cases where the answers did not include the most relevant context. Instead, they referred to content that was only weakly related to the question. To address this, a post-retrieval re-ranking was incorporated. Inspired by two key studies [13,14], a *Re-ranker* agent based on GPT-4o mini was developed and guided using a one-shot prompting technique. This agent reorders the retrieved chunks according to their semantic similarity to the query. Then, the top three chunks are selected as the device-relevant context for the query. The **Patient Context Retrieval Pipeline** (4) incorporates a pre-retrieval agent, the *Mediator*. The Mediator acts as a crucial bridge between CT protocol-focused user queries and the patient context database. It is essential because most user questions focus on CT protocol adjustment, not explicitly patient conditions. As a result, directly using the query to retrieve context from the patient vector database is ineffective. Powered by GPT-4o mini, the Mediator is guided to analyze the user's query and return a list of general relevant health conditions. The Mediator's output is then converted into a vector and compared against the patient vector database using L2 distance. By applying a distance threshold, the top five most relevant contexts regarding the patient's condition are retrieved.

As shown in (5), the **Model Prompt** is created using the query and the extracted context from the databases. Together with the system message, the prompt is delivered to the LLM. The generated answer includes both plain text and required tags. Subsequently, the answer is rendered in the user interface. To this end, the model response is processed in the frontend to convert tags into actionable links, enabling the user to adjust the scan workflow, or navigate to the relevant patient condition extracted from clinical reports.

## 2.3 Evaluation

For evaluation, we considered two question categories: independently asked one-shot questions, and subsequent follow-up questions based on a previous answer or query. In each evaluation round, we asked the chatbot 130âĂŞ150 questions related to five patients, spanning seven categories: parameter adjustment, enabling/disabling features, patient details, invalid inputs, recommended settings, workflow information, and device suitability. Notably, multiple valid answers may exist for a single query. To this end, during the evaluation phase we leveraged a concept we denote as **Expectation Notes**, which are manually created for each query and specify the information and tags that must be included in the answer and their respective format. The expectation note serves as a reference to evaluate the generated answer for the corresponding query. We then developed an **Evaluator Agent** that aims to automate this process. This agent is based on GPT-4o mini and operates under detailed instructions. The instruction outlines all evaluation criteria and emphasizes that the LLM first provides a rationale before assigning a score to each criterion. The agent receives the query, all retrieved context, the chatbot-generated answer, and the corresponding expectation note. It then returns a structured output containing justifications and scores ranging from 0 to 100%.

## 3 Results

### 3.1 Final System Performance

Table 1 presents the chatbot's performance using GPT-4o and GPT-4o mini. In both experiments, the chatbot demonstrated consistently high performance, implying robustness of the configuration and the effectiveness of the applied prompting techniques. The GPT-4o-based chatbot demonstrated slightly superior performance in aligning with predefined expectations and producing more complete answers, matching our initial expectations.

### 3.2 Ablation Study

As previously stated, the chatbot's final configuration is composed of three components: 1) a RAG system that incorporates role assignment, task definitions, tag introductions, and both device- and patient-relevant context; 2) instruction prompting to guide the LLM on how to utilize the context, which tags to apply, and where they should appear in the answers for each kind of question; 3) few-shot prompting by providing ten question-answer examples to demonstrate how the LLM should use tags in the correct format within its responses. We conducted an ablation study to evaluate how the chatbot's performance changes when these prompting techniques are excluded. The results are presented in Fig. 2, which compare the performance of each configuration against the full approach using GPT-4o mini. As shown in the figure, although *without few-shot prompting* results in lower performance compared to the full model, the chatbot

**Table 1.** Average performance of the final prompt across all criteria with respect to the *Expectation Note* using GPT-4o vs. GPT-4o mini (in %)

| Criterion | Score | | Difference |
|---|---|---|---|
| | GPT-4o mini | GPT-4 | |
| Expectation Matching | 95.01 | **98.28** | 3.28 |
| Completeness | 95.33 | **98.01** | 2.68 |
| Application Tagging Accuracy | 96.16 | **97.98** | 1.82 |
| Answer Relevancy | 97.07 | **98.85** | 1.79 |
| Linguistic Accuracy | 99.75 | **100** | 0.25 |
| Patient Context Relevance | 99.84 | **99.92** | 0.08 |
| Device Context Relevance | 99.81 | **99.87** | 0.06 |
| Device Context Tagging Accuracy | **100** | 100 | - |
| Patient Context Tagging Accuracy | **100** | 100 | - |

still outperforms other ablation configurations. In the majority of cases, relevant tags were present, but often formatted incorrectly. Further, the answers did not fully or accurately reflect the extracted context. This highlights that few-shot examples clarify the desired answer format for LLMs, demonstrating how to use extracted context and required tagging.

In the second experiment, *without instruction prompting*, the chatbot showed decreased performance across all evaluation criteria. The chatbot exhibited inconsistencies in generating responses with appropriate tags and in effectively utilizing the extracted context. This illustrates the more critical role of instructions compared to few-shot examples in helping the chatbot understand how to

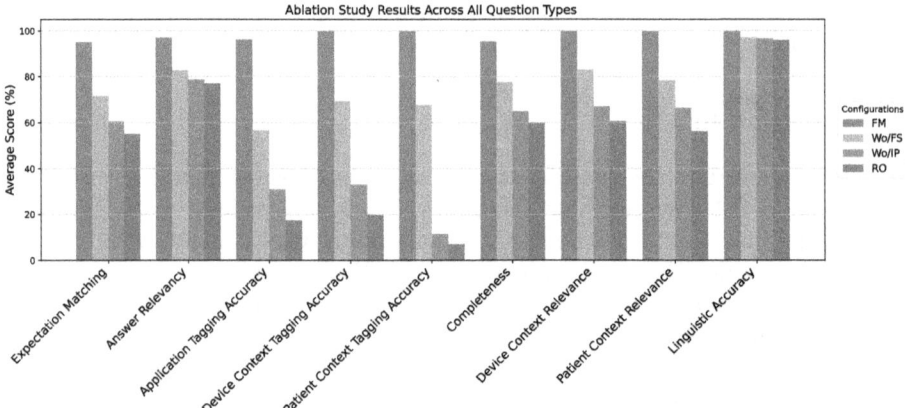

**Fig. 2.** Ablation study results across evaluation criteria for all questions types. Configurations: FM= Full Model, Wo/FS= Without Few-Shot Prompting, Wo/IP= Without Instruction Prompting, RO= RAG-Only.

generate answers for different types of questions, specifying when and which tags should be included.

Finally, in the *RAG-only* setting, we excluded both few-shot and instruction prompting. While the responses were relevant to the query, they showed poor integration of the extracted context and failed to incorporate the required tags to adjust the scan workflow or refer to device- or patient-relevant context. Overall, the chatbot's performance was notably worse than in the other configurations.

Expectedly, linguistic accuracy was high across all tested scenarios and deemed only slightly more accurate with the full approach.

## 4 Discussion

This study introduces a chatbot-based intelligent CT workflow assistant, leveraging an advanced RAG framework that integrates device-specific technical, and patient-specific clinical context. By incorporating prompting techniques, the proposed method yields accurate responses with actionable links to relevant acquisition and postprocessing settings. Unlike prior work that largely focused on patient-centric factors, this approach explicitly accounts for scanner capabilities, thereby enhancing the clinical applicability for automated protocol guidance. Further, it improves transparency by referencing device documentation, clinical indications, and prior diagnostic findings. An LLM-based evaluation framework was developed to assess the chatbot's performance, with our assistant achieving up to 98.3% alignment with predefined expectations using GPT-4o. An ablation analysis confirmed the critical role of the applied prompting techniques. Collectively, these findings underscore the viability of LLM-based assistants in supporting context-sensitive decision-making processes in radiological workflows.

The study faced several key challenges. The selection of a suitable LLM proved difficult; the model needed both extensive healthcare knowledge and strong contextual reasoning to produce coherent responses. Crucially, its ability to handle a large volume of simultaneous contextual information significantly limited our options.

Another difficulty arose in prompt engineering. We found it challenging to balance the need for precise instructions, i.e. to ensure accurate, formatted responses, with flexibility [15] to avoid overly rigid outputs. This balance was ultimately achieved through iterative refinement of our prompts. Finally, while extensive evaluation by human experts was considered desirable yet impractical, we addressed this by creating an LLM-based evaluator. Through iterative testing and refinement of evaluation prompts, the system provided reliable assessments and proved to be the most practical solution for our study. This work suggests several directions for future development. Fine-tuning an open-source LLM to generate tagged answers in a consistent style could reduce reliance on lengthy system prompts, lowering processing demands and enabling the use of models with smaller context windows. Though we utilized unstructured text reports, real clinical environments incorporate diverse data sources and formats. Expanding the context retrieval pipeline into a multi-agent system capable of accessing various clinical data sources could further enhance the relevance and accuracy of generated responses.

# References

1. Kalra, A., Chakraborty, A., Fine, B., Reicher, J.: Machine learning for automation of radiology protocols for quality and efficiency improvement. J. Am. Coll. Radiol. **17**(9), 1149–1158 (2020)
2. López-Úbeda, P., Díaz-Galiano, M.C., Martín-Noguerol, T., Luna, A., Ureña-López, L.A., Martin-Valdivia, M.T.: Automatic medical protocol classification using machine learning approaches. Comput. Methods Programs Biomed. **200**, 105939 (2021)
3. Chillakuru, Y.R., et al.: Development and web deployment of an automated neuroradiology MRI protocoling tool with natural language processing. BMC Med. Inform. Decis. Mak. **21**, 1–10 (2021)
4. Bhayana, R.: Chatbots and large language models in radiology: a practical primer for clinical and research applications. Radiology **310**(1), e232756 (2024)
5. Kofler, J.M., Cody, D.D., Morin, R.L.: CT protocol review and optimization. J. Am. Coll. Radiol. **11**(3), 267–270 (2014)
6. Rau, A., et al.: A context-based chatbot surpasses radiologists and generic ChatGPT in following the ACR appropriateness guidelines. Radiology **308**(1), e230970 (2023)
7. Gertz, R.J., et al.: GPT-4 for automated determination of radiologic study and protocol based on radiology request forms: a feasibility study. Radiology **307**(5), e230877 (2023)
8. Huang, L., et al.: A survey on hallucination in large language models: principles, taxonomy, challenges, and open questions. ACM Trans. Inf. Syst. **43**(2), 1–55 (2025)
9. Sanu, E., Amudaa, T.K., Bhat, P., Dinesh, G., Chate, A.U.K., Kumar, R.: Limitations of large language models. In 2024 8th International Conference on Computational System and Information Technology for Sustainable Solutions (CSITSS), pp. 1-6. IEEE (2024)
10. Lewis, P., et al.: Retrieval-augmented generation for knowledge-intensive NLP tasks. In: Advances in Neural Information Processing Systems, vol. 33, pp. 9459–9474 (2020)
11. Sahoo, P., Singh, A.K., Saha, S., Jain, V., Mondal, S., Chadha, A.: A systematic survey of prompt engineering in large language models: techniques and applications. arXiv preprint arXiv:2402.07927 (2024)
12. Li, C., et al.:Large language models understand and can be enhanced by emotional stimuli. arXiv preprint arXiv:2307.11760 (2023)
13. Sun, W., et al.: Is ChatGPT good at search? investigating large language models as re-ranking agents. arXiv preprint arXiv:2304.09542 (2023)
14. Chang, C.Y., et al.: MAIN-RAG: multi-agent filtering retrieval-augmented generation. arXiv preprint arXiv:2501.00332 (2024)
15. Geroimenko, V.: The Essential Guide to Prompt Engineering: Key Principles. Challenges, and Security Risks. Springer Nature, Techniques (2025)

# SIGMA: Auto-Regressive VLM for Automated Radiology Report Generation from Longitudinal 3D CT Volumes

Khang C. Nguyen[1(✉)], Cheng Wang[1], Zong X. Shi[1], Yue Heng[1], Chuan Y. Qi[1], Masahiro Oda[1,2], and Kensaku Mori[1,2,3]

[1] Graduate School of Informatics, Nagoya University, Nagoya, Japan
khangncbh@gmail.com
[2] Information Technology Center, Nagoya University, Nagoya, Japan
[3] Research Center for Medical Bigdata, National Institute of Informatics, Tokyo, Japan

**Abstract.** Globally, approximately 375 million CT scans are performed annually, with Japan performing around 30 million scans, leading in scan density. Radiologists have to face a significant workload, which results in delays and reduced diagnostic quality due to understaffing. To mitigate these issues, artificial intelligence (AI) is being explored for generating radiology reports, aiming to reduce workload and minimize human error. This study focuses on the use of vision language models (VLMs) to integrate textual and visual data. Most VLMs are designed for 2D images, while the few existing 3D VLMs either lack longitudinal volume integration or clinical histories, and none are tailored for Japanese report generation, which is further complicated by the complexity of the language. In this research, we introduce SIGMA, designed to automatically generate Japanese radiology findings reports from longitudinal 3D CT volumes, guided by medical expert instruction. Our model integrates the state-of-the-art language model, Gemma 2, with the Swin Transformer technique to enhance the efficiency of 3D image processing. We trained SIGMA using a large-scale longitudinal CT dataset, quantitatively and qualitatively evaluated its performance. The results are promising and establish the first baseline for future research in Japanese radiology report generation.

**Keywords:** VLM · Longitudinal Data · Clinical Histories · Radiology Report · 3D CT

## 1 Introduction

Approximately 375 million computed tomography (CT) scans are conducted globally annually, with an annual growth rate of 3–4%. Japan, characterized by its extensive access to CT scanners, boasts the highest density of such equipment worldwide, resulting in the execution of approximately 30 million CT scans each year [1]. Radiologists are tasked with interpreting CT volumes obtained from multiple examinations for the purposes of diagnosis, treatment planning, and patient monitoring. This process is inherently time-consuming [3] and necessitates the meticulous examination of various anatomical structures at different intervals [4]. Consequently, this imposes a significant burden on the already understaffed radiology workforce, leading to delays in clinical decision-making and a decline in diagnostic quality [6]. Hence, there is a compelling impetus to employ artificial intelligence in the generation of radiology reports, aiming to alleviate the interpretative workload and minimize human error [2].

To address this task, it is crucial to integrate both textual and visual modalities, emphasizing the potential of vision language models (VLMs). Although numerous efforts have been made to develop VLMs for report generation, most focus on 2D images, such as single slice of CT or X-ray images [11]. In contrast, the limited number of 3D VLMs [11] either do not incorporate historical volumes from previous visits or do not utilize clinical historical data, which are typically crucial in medical settings. Furthermore, none of these studies employing 3D CT have specifically aimed at generating reports in Japanese, a language with a complex writing system and highly agglutinative nature.

In response to the identified issue, we introduce SIGMA, designed to autonomously generate Japanese radiology findings reports from longitudinal 3D CT volumes and expert medical instruction. SIGMA, which stands for Swin Transformer Integrated Gemma for Medical Assistant, is constructed upon the Gemma 2 architecture [13,14] to enhance the model's capacity for capturing extended contexts. This is further augmented by the integration of a 3D Swin-Transformer module, serving as the vision model to facilitate efficient processing of 3D volumes. Our contributions can be summarized as:

- We introduce SIGMA, a VLM designed to enhance the comprehension of longitudinal 3D CT volumes and medical expert instructions.
- We assess SIGMA's performance using quantitative metrics, including Natural Language Generation (NLG) and Clinical Efficacy (CE), to demonstrate our model's potential efficacy.
- In addressing the challenge of generating reports in Japanese, SIGMA represents the pioneering effort to produce Japanese reports directly from 3D CT images, establishes a baseline for future research efforts.

## 2 Method

### 2.1 Vision Language Model

SIGMA accepts two longitudinal CT volumes and an instruction containing clinical historical information (e.g. postoperative rectal cancer, after gallectomy, ...) as input, outputs a radiology findings report in the text modality. The network architecture comprises four key components: 3D vision encoder; adapter; text encoder; large language model (LLM), as illustrated in Fig. 1. The input CT volumes share the same 3D vision encoder and adapter. Furthermore, the vision feature and text embedding vectors are concatenated before being fed to the language model as a text embedding vector.

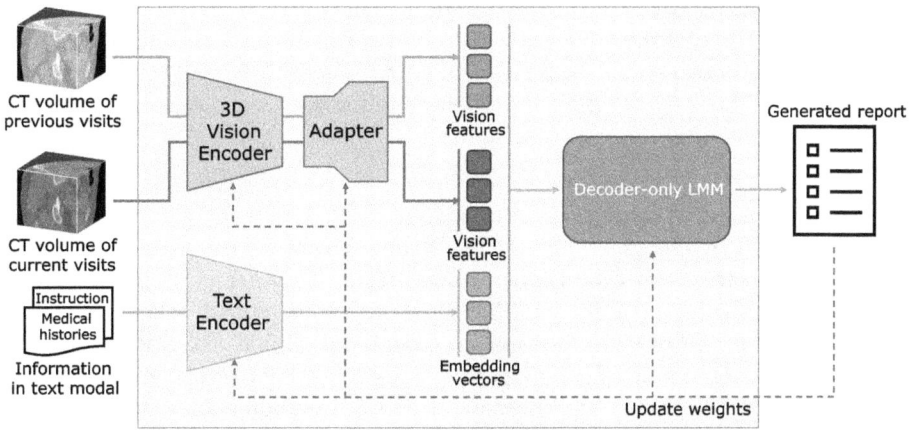

**Fig. 1.** Structure of the proposed method. Word embedding and vision feature embedding vectors are concatenated before being passed to the LLM as an input embedding vector. The solid lines represent the inference process, while the dashed lines represent the weight update process.

**3D Vision Encoder:** We utilize 3D Swin Transformers [12] to extract visual features from input CT volumes. The encoder receives a single channel input volume $\mathbf{X}_v \in \mathbb{R}^{H \times W \times D}$. First, we employ a patch partitioning layer to divide the volume to 3D tokens of size $2 \times 2 \times 2$, which are then projected into a 48-dimensional space through an embedding layer. Then we pass these embedding vectors through four stages, each comprising two transformer blocks to obtain a bottleneck feature $\mathbf{H}_v$ with resolution $\frac{H}{32} \times \frac{W}{32} \times \frac{D}{32}$ and embedding dimension of 768 [12], which is subsequently passed to the adapter for further processing.

**Adapter:** The adapter is employed to align the dimensionality between the vision encoder and the language model. This initially receives the output $\mathbf{H}_v$ of the vision encoder, and flattens it along the spatial dimension to obtain the feature $\mathbf{H}'_v \in \mathbb{R}^{L_v \times 768}$, where $L_v = \frac{H \times W \times D}{32^3}$. Subsequently, the adapter transforms these vision features into vectors $\mathbf{E}_v$ that match the dimension $d_{model}$ of the word embeddings, which are then integrated into the vectors fed into the language model. Following the approach in [8], a fully connected layer $\mathbf{W}$ is employed to map the vision features to the word embedding space. Mathematically, this is represented as

$$\mathbf{E}_v = \mathbf{W}\mathbf{H}'_v \qquad (1)$$

This implies that each volume $\mathbf{X}_v$ is considered as a sequence of tokens with length $L_v$.

**Text Encoder:** The text encoder converts the input instruction into word embedding vectors that capture the semantic meaning of the words and their relationships. Specifically, the input text is broken down into words or pieces of words, which correspond to an ID called tokens. Subsequently, these tokens are embedded into vector space by an embedding layer. The output of the text encoder is denoted as $\mathbf{E}_t$.

**Large Language Model:** We employ Gemma 2, a text-to-text, decoder-only LLM developed by Google. This model features a context length of 8192 tokens and utilizes Rotary Position Embedding [13,14]. Two primary innovations in Gemma 2 facilitate its ability to handle long sequences of tokens: Grouped Query Attention (GQA) and Alternating Local and Global Attention [14]. GQA enhances traditional multi-head attention by aggregating queries, enabling faster processing and improving the model efficiency in managing extensive token sequences. Alternating Local and Global Attention, on the other hand, alternates between a local sliding window attention and global attention in every other layer, rather than considering all words in a text simultaneously. This dual approach allows the model to effectively comprehend both the immediate context and the overall meaning of the text efficiently [14].

## 2.2 Generation Strategy

We employ greedy search as the generation strategy for our framework. After trained, the model generate one token at each step. At step $t$, we select the token $\mathbf{y}_t$ that has the highest probability given the previous $t-1$ tokens $\{\mathbf{y}_1, \mathbf{y}_2, ..., \mathbf{y}_{t-1}\}$. In formula form, this is expressed as

$$\mathbf{y}_t = \arg\max_{\mathbf{y}} P(\mathbf{y} \mid \mathbf{y}_1, ..., \mathbf{y}_{t-1}) \tag{2}$$

This process is repeated until a stopping criterion is met, i.e. either generating an end-of-sequence token or reaching a maximum length.

## 2.3 Dataset

We used data collected from seven distinct medical institutions over the period from 2021 to 2023, resulting in a comprehensive clinical dataset comprising 13,000 independent patients. The collected data specifically include CT scan images and corresponding radiology reports. These data were utilized to construct a longitudinal dataset for the purposes of training and evaluation.

**CT Scan Data and Corresponding Report:** Each CT scan session was assigned a unique ID linking it to the corresponding report, study date/time, and patient. Each session included multiple series (e.g., non-contrast, contrast-enhanced), but only one was selected per visit (see Sect. 3.1). Radiology reports, written in Japanese by experts, were limited to the findings section, following [4]. This section may include exam method, previous visits, patient's clinical histories, and the main text, which can contain abbreviations or English terms. As information beyond the main text are accessible in clinical settings, the model was tasked with generating only the main text.

**Longitudinal Data Set:** We assumed that all reports with comparisons were based on two consecutive visits. Using the ID of the CTs, we identified two consecutive examinations for the same patient. We constructed a longitudinal dataset comprising pairs of CT volumes from consecutive examinations and a corresponding findings report from the subsequent examination. The training dataset consisted of 35,000 such sets, while the testing dataset included 6,500 sets of longitudinal volumes and their associated findings reports.

### 2.4 Matching Rate for Clinical Efficacy Evaluation

To assess the clinical efficacy of the model, an independent language model is employed to identify commonalities between reports generated by SIGMA and those authored by radiologists. Specifically, the language model is prompted to include 1) $N_f$ findings of SIGMA's output and 2) $N_m$ similar findings between two reports in its output under a designed format. Subsequently, the regular expression is utilized to parse these information. We defined the matching rate $r_m \in [0,1]$ as follows

$$r_m = \frac{N_m}{N_f} \quad (3)$$

If every findings of the model are similar to the expert findings, this ratio is 1. Conversely, if no findings are similar, $r_m$ is 0.

## 3 Experiment

### 3.1 Data Pre-processing

In this experiment, we selected series with a volume resolution of 512×512 pixels on the axial plane. Due to computational resource constraints, the number of slices per volume was limited to 96. To minimize the impact of resizing, we selected series with a number of slices closest to 96. CT values were restricted to a range of -500 Hounsfield Units (H.U.) to 250 H.U. and normalized to the [0,1] range prior to input into the vision encoder.

## 3.2 Experiment Settings

The feature dimension of the language model was set to $d_{model} = 3584$. Pretrained weights provided by [12] were utilized for the vision encoder, while weights from the model named gemma-2-9b-it [14] were used for the text encoder and the LLM as initial weights. During the training phase, all weights were subject to updates. The Adam optimizer was utilized, with the hyperparameters $\beta_1$ and $\beta_2$ hyperparameters set to 0.9 and 0.99, respectively. The cross-entropy loss function was applied, with a batch size of 1 and a learning rate of 0.0001. We employed the Qwen2.5-72B-Instruct model [15] for (1) pre-processing the findings report (separating the main text from the original report), and (2) analyze the SIGMA's output to perform CE evaluations, based on its performance observed in our preliminary experiments. Inference using a single H100 GPU with a 300-token limit averaged 17.2 s per findings report.

**Table 1.** Comparison of the output of SIGMA compared to the findings written by a radiologist. Similar findings are highlighted in green while difference findings are highlighted in red.

| | |
|---|---|
| Input | 所見文を生成してください。左下葉肺腺癌加療中 |
| (Translated) | Please generate the report. Currently undergoing treatment for adenocarcinoma of the left lower lobe of the lung. |
| Model Output | 左肺上葉の原発巣は前回より縮小しています。右肺に放射性肺臓炎疑いあり。前回同様です。右肺中葉末梢の濃厚影は前回同様です。炎症後変化を疑います。右肺門、縦隔L転移腫大は縮小を維持しています。右肺門や縦隔、右鎖骨上窩リンパ節転移も縮小を維持しています。右胸水は減少。肝転移を疑うSOLなし。肝嚢胞あり。副腎腫大なし。明らかな骨転移巣なし。 |
| (Translated) | The primary lesion in the left upper lung lobe has shrunk since the last time. Suspected radiation pneumonitis in the right lung, same as before. The dense shadow in the peripheral right middle lobe is unchanged, suspected post-inflammatory change. The enlarged lymph nodes in the right hilum and mediastinum have maintained their reduction. The metastases in the right hilum, mediastinum, and right supraclavicular lymph nodes have also maintained their reduction. Right pleural effusion has decreased. No suspected liver metastasis. Liver cyst present. No adrenal enlargement. No obvious bone metastasis. |
| Expert written | 原発巣や両肺の複数の肺転移は前回同様で縮小維持しています。リンパ節転移は縮小維持し有意なリンパ節腫大なし。肝転移と両副腎転移は縮小を維持して不明瞭です。新規肝転移なし。骨盤骨の骨硬化は前回同様です。その他、新たな骨転移を疑う病変は認めません。胸水なし。胆、膵、脾、腎に異常なし。腹水少量出現しています。 |
| (Translated) | The primary tumor and multiple lung metastases are stable and reduced as before. Lymph node metastases are also reduced with no significant enlargement. Liver and adrenal metastases remain reduced and unclear. No new liver metastases. Pelvic bone sclerosis is unchanged. No new bone metastases suspected. No pleural effusion. No abnormalities in the gallbladder, pancreas, spleen, or kidneys. A small amount of ascites is present. |

## 4 Result and Discussion

Table 1 shows a qualitative example of an output from SIGMA and an expert-authored report. The model-generated report uses medical terminology and includes findings on metastasis and other changes that closely resemble those in the radiologist-authored report. However, each report contains distinct findings not mentioned in the other. Specifically, in the example shown in Table 1, model-generated report indicates a reduction in the amount of pleural effusion, whereas the expert asserts that no pleural effusion is present.

To quantitatively assess the SIGMA's effectiveness, we employed NLG and CE metrics. The NLG metrics included: BLEU-n (BL-n) [10], with n ranging from 1 to 4 to measure word overlap; METEOR (M) [5], which considers synonym usage and word order; ROUGE-L (R) [7], based on the Longest Common Subsequence; and BERTScore (B) [16], which evaluates semantic content. For the CE metrics, we utilized: $r_m$, as detailed in Sect. 2.4, and GREEN (G) [9], which assesses the ratio between correct and error findings. Both NLG and CE evaluations were conducted under two conditions: with and without patient treatment progress information included in the instructions. The results are presented in Table 2. For reference, we have also directly cited the evaluation results from the original paper of the previous research. It is important to note that the prior work was conducted and assessed in English, whereas our study was conducted in Japanese, which may render direct comparisons less equitable.

**Table 2.** The quantitative evaluation demonstrates the efficacy of our SIGMA model relative to prior studies. The "+" symbol is used to denote results where additional information has been included into the prompt

| Method | NLG | | | | | | | CE | |
|---|---|---|---|---|---|---|---|---|---|
| | BL-1 | BL-2 | BL-3 | BL-4 | M | RL | B-F1 | $r_m$ | G |
| CT2RepLong [4] | **0.374** | **0.327** | **0.304** | **0.401** | 0.285 | 0.263 | – | – | – |
| SIGMA (Ours) | 0.313 | 0.243 | 0.183 | 0.147 | 0.230 | 0.253 | 0.730 | 0.306 | 0.272 |
| SIGMA+ (Ours) | 0.318 | 0.247 | 0.196 | 0.202 | **0.322** | **0.287** | **0.746** | **0.353** | **0.361** |

Table 2 demonstrates that providing treatment progress through expert instruction prompts enables the model to better understand the context, thereby enhancing the quality of the output report. Despite the low BL-n score, the M and RL scores are relatively high, suggesting that while the generated text may not contain many exact matches with the reference text, it still effectively conveys the intended meaning. Additionally, the $r_m$ value indicates that approximately one-third of the model's findings are similar to the reference text, as observed in Table 1. The GREEN score is lower than $r_m$ possibly due to its penalization of missing findings that are present in the reference.

Despite these promising results, several limitations must be acknowledged. The lack of established baselines and publicly available benchmarks for Japanese-language radiology report generation restricts comprehensive evaluation, which is critical for clinical implementation. Moreover, using a fixed number of slices may limit the model's ability to capture spatial dependencies across slices.

## 5 Conclusions

We presented SIGMA, a novel 3D VLM that integrates the Swin Transformer for 3D medical image analysis with the Gemma 2 language model, enabling efficient processing of longitudinal CT volumes for automatic generation of radiology reports. SIGMA uniquely targets Japanese-language radiology report generation - representing the first such application for 3D CT data and tracking disease progression over time. Future research will aim to address the challenges regarding evaluation, further refine the model, and investigate its applicability to real-world clinical settings.

**Acknowledgments.** Parts of this work was supported by the Cross-ministerial Strategic Innovation Promotion Program (SIP) (Contract Number SIP2023E2_3), JSPS KAKENHI (Grant Number 24H00720), and JST [Moonshot R&D][Grant Number JPMJMS2214].

**Disclosure of Interests.** The authors declare that there are no competing interests.

## References

1. Aoyama, T., et al.: A cross-national investigation of CT, MRI, PET, mammography, and radiation therapy resources and utilization. Jpn. J. Radiol. 1–8 (2024)
2. Blankemeier, L., et al.: Merlin: a vision language foundation model for 3D computed tomography. Res. Square rs–3 (2024)
3. Chen, Z., Bie, Y., Jin, H., Chen, H.: Large language model with region-guided referring and grounding for CT report generation. arXiv preprint arXiv:2411.15539 (2024)
4. Hamamci, I.E., Er, S., Menze, B.: CT2Rep: automated radiology report generation for 3D medical imaging. In: International Conference on Medical Image Computing and Computer-Assisted Intervention, pp. 476–486. Springer (2024)
5. Lavie, A., Denkowski, M.J.: The METEOR metric for automatic evaluation of machine translation. Mach. Transl. **23**, 105–115 (2009)
6. Lee, C.S., Nagy, P.G., Weaver, S.J., Newman-Toker, D.E.: Cognitive and system factors contributing to diagnostic errors in radiology. Am. J. Roentgenol. **201**(3), 611–617 (2013)
7. Lin, C.Y.: ROUGE: a package for automatic evaluation of summaries. In: Text Summarization Branches Out, pp. 74–81 (2004)
8. Liu, H., Li, C., Wu, Q., Lee, Y.J.: Visual instruction tuning. Adv. Neural. Inf. Process. Syst. **36**, 34892–34916 (2023)
9. Ostmeier, S., et al.: GREEN: Generative radiology report evaluation and error notation. arXiv preprint arXiv:2405.03595 (2024)
10. Papineni, K., Roukos, S., Ward, T., Zhu, W.J.: BLEU: a method for automatic evaluation of machine translation. In: Proceedings of the 40th Annual Meeting of the Association for Computational Linguistics, pp. 311–318 (2002)

11. Sloan, P., Clatworthy, P., Simpson, E., Mirmehdi, M.: Automated radiology report generation: a review of recent advances. IEEE Rev. Biomed. Eng. **18**, 368–387 (2024)
12. Tang, Y., et al.: Self-supervised pre-training of swin transformers for 3D medical image analysis. In: Proceedings of the IEEE/CVF Conference on Computer Vision and Pattern Recognition, pp. 20730–20740 (2022)
13. Team, G., et al.: Gemma: Open models based on Gemini research and technology. arXiv preprint arXiv:2403.08295 (2024)
14. Team, G., et al.: Gemma 2: Improving open language models at a practical size. arXiv preprint arXiv:2408.00118 (2024)
15. Yang, A., et al.: Qwen2. 5 technical report. arXiv preprint arXiv:2412.15115 (2024)
16. Zhang, T., Kishore, V., Wu, F., Weinberger, K.Q., Artzi, Y.: BERTScore: Evaluating text generation with BERT. arXiv preprint arXiv:1904.09675 (2019)

# Specialised or Generic? Tokenization Choices for Radiology Language Models

Hermione Warr[1](✉), Wentian Xu[1], Harry Anthony[1], Yasin Ibrahim[1], Daniel R. McGowan[2,3], and Konstantinos Kamnitsas[1]

[1] Department of Engineering Science, University of Oxford, Oxford, UK
{hermione.warr,wentian.xu,harry.anthony,yasin.ibrahim,
konstantinos.kamnitsas}@eng.ox.ac.uk
[2] Department of Oncology, University of Oxford, Oxford, UK
[3] Department of Medical Physics and Clinical Engineering, OUH NHS FT, Oxford, UK

**Abstract.** The vocabulary used by language models (LM) - defined by the tokenizer - plays a key role in text generation quality. However, its impact remains under-explored in radiology. In this work, we address this gap by systematically comparing general, medical, and domain-specific tokenizers on the task of radiology report summarisation across three imaging modalities. We also investigate scenarios with and without LM pre-training on PubMed abstracts. Our findings demonstrate that medical and domain-specific vocabularies outperformed widely used natural language alternatives when models are trained from scratch. Pre-training partially mitigates performance differences between tokenizers, whilst the domain-specific tokenizers achieve the most favourable results. Domain-specific tokenizers also reduce memory requirements due to smaller vocabularies and shorter sequences. These results demonstrate that adapting the vocabulary of LMs to the clinical domain provides practical benefits, including improved performance and reduced computational demands, making such models more accessible and effective for both research and real-world healthcare settings. Code available at: GitHub.

**Keywords:** Radiology Report Generation · Vocabulary · Language Model

## 1 Introduction

Radiologists are facing mounting challenges managing the growing volume of imaging data. The integration of artificial intelligence (AI) for assisting radiology report generation has gained attention as a potential solution. The advent

---

**Supplementary Information** The online version contains supplementary material available at https://doi.org/10.1007/978-3-032-07502-4_8.

of Transformers [14] significantly advanced language models (LMs), prompting interest in their application to radiology reporting [9]. As LMs become increasingly accessible and capable, adapting them for clinical use remains non-trivial. A key challenge lies in ensuring factual accuracy in generating complex radiological text under computational constraints. Strategies to address this include adapting model architectures [9] and biomedical domain pre-training [4]. An important, yet often overlooked component, is the *tokenizer*, which defines the *vocabulary* the model operates on. Tokenization determines how text is represented in an LM, influencing both model performance and computational efficiency.

In prior work, most radiology LMs were built on general-purpose tokenizers trained on natural language corpora, such as those from GPT-2 or LLaMA2 [9]. Others use generic biomedical vocabularies like PubMedBERT, trained on PubMed abstracts [4], and some models were developed with a specific medical dataset vocabulary [2,9]. Clinical text diverges from general English in syntax, terminology, and structure. It includes specialised vocabulary, abbreviations, and structured content like diagnostic codes and measurements. This can challenge general tokenizers and limit downstream performance. Moreover, most studies focused on chest X-ray reports, while other modalities remain under-explored [5,9]. This issue is compounded by the computational demands of large LMs, limiting research in resource-constrained settings, especially on 3D scans like PET-CTs. This motivates research into smaller, task-specific models that require less memory and compute compared to large-scale general purpose models. The choice of tokenizer - and by extension, vocabulary - affects all of the above factors. It determines how efficiently medical language is represented, impacting both model performance and computational requirements.

In this study we develop a range of domain-specific and biomedical vocabularies, and compare them against general natural-language vocabularies for the task of radiology report summarisation. We also examine scenarios with and without LM pre-training. We assess performance and memory requirements across 3 datasets that span 3 imaging modalities: X-rays using MIMIC-CXR [6], CTs with CT-RATE [5], and a private oncology PET-CT database. Our findings demonstrate that data-specific tokenization improves both performance and memory efficiency across all datasets when LMs are trained from scratch. These insights inform best practices for developing radiology LMs, particularly in resource constrained settings.

## 2 Methodology

**Problem Setting and Report Summarisation Task:** The task of generating a textual sequence $T$ can be framed as estimating the conditional distribution $p(T)$ as product of conditional probabilities, $p(T) = \prod_{s=1}^{S} p(T_s \mid T_{<s}; \theta)$. Here $T$ is modelled as a sequence of word tokens $\{T_1, ..., T_S\}$, $T_{<s}$ is the set of tokens preceding $T_s$, and $\theta$ is the model parameters. A *tokenizer* maps input text to a set of $S$ token vectors $\{T_{tok,s}\}_{1:S} \in \mathbb{R}^{S \times V}$, where $S$ is the sequence length and $V$ the size of the *vocabulary*. Each $T_{tok,s}$ is embedded by a linear layer, so $T_{emb} = f_{T,emb}(T_{tok}) \in \mathbb{R}^{S \times D}$ is a set of S token embeddings with dimensionality $D$.

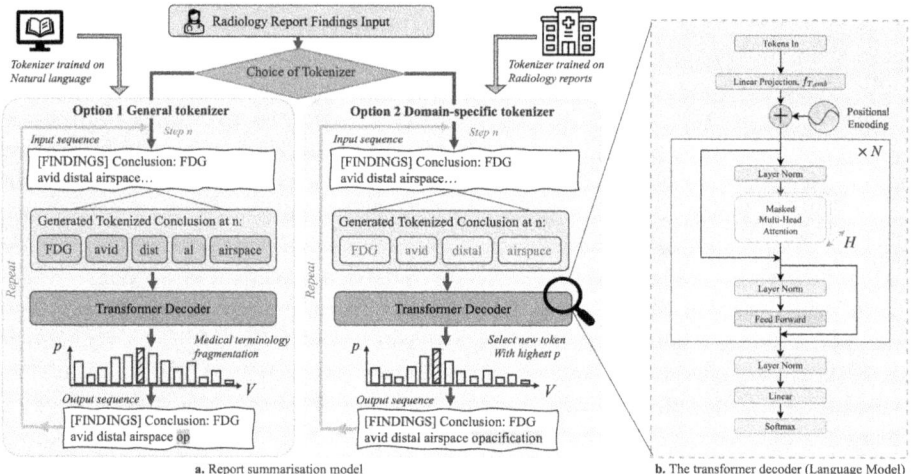

**Fig. 1.** (a) An inference step for radiology report summarisation: predicting the *Conclusion* from the *Findings* section. The tokenized Findings and previously generated Conclusion tokens are passed to the autoregressive model (b), which outputs a vocabulary distribution to predict the next token. A general tokenizer requires more tokens and longer sequences, as out-of-vocabulary words (e.g., distal, opacification) are fragmented.

The token embeddings are passed into a Transformer decoder with $N$ attention blocks, each with $H$ heads [14]. This outputs a probability distribution over the $V$ vocabulary tokens, indicating the most likely next token in the sequence.

We evaluate the impact of the tokenizer on the task of *radiology report summarisation* (Fig. 1). Specifically, we input the *Findings* section of a radiology report to the model. We then train the LM to generate the *Conclusion* of the report, which summarises the main findings.

**Tokenizers in Depth:** Tokenization is a preprocessing step in NLP that converts raw text into a sequence of smaller units called tokens, which serve as the atomic inputs to LMs. Tokenizers define how text is broken down and map character sequences to a fixed *vocabulary* - a set of unique tokens *learned* from a training corpus *prior* to LM training. Without loss of generality, we focus on *Byte Pair Encoding (BPE)* tokenizers [12], a widely-used tokenization algorithm. Training a BPE tokenizer involves learning a series of merge operations from a text corpus. This process begins with a dictionary consisting of all individual characters present in the corpus. The most frequent adjacent pairs of symbols are iteratively merged to form new subword tokens, until either all words in the corpus are included or a predefined vocabulary size is reached [12]. The result is an ordered list of merge operations and a vocabulary, both of which are required at inference time to tokenize new inputs. To *apply* a trained BPE tokenizer, the input text is first split into individual characters. The tokenizer then applies the learned merge operations in order, combining frequent adjacent pairs into subwords until no further merges are possible. The vocabulary learned by the tokenizer depends on the text the tokenizer is trained on. We define *domain-specific tokenizers* as those trained exclusively on text from a single domain, such as radiology reports, and *general tokenizers* as those trained on broad, multi-domain corpora. Given a maximum size of allowed vocabulary, training a tokenizer with larger, more varied text, results in vocabularies where rare words are not represented, and instead broken down into smaller subword tokens (fragmentation). This trade-off is illustrated in Fig. 1a, which highlights how the same input is tokenized under different vocabularies. Once trained, the tokenizer is applied to the training data, and the resulting tokens are used to train an LM.

**Vocabulary, Sequence Length, and Required Memory:** Properties of the tokenizer affect the memory required by LMs. Studying this can inform the choice of appropriate tokenizer, or enable training with more limited hardware. To this end, we derive an estimation of GPU memory $M$ required during the training of a Transformer-based LM with the general architecture shown in Fig. 1. This estimate depends on the tokenizer's vocabulary size $V$, input sequence length $S$, batch size $B$, model hidden dimension $D$, number of heads $H$, and number of blocks $N$. We can approximate the memory $M$ required by such an LM, in one training step, as a sum of four components:

$$M = M_{\text{act}} + M_\theta + M^\theta_{\text{grad}} + M_{\text{opt}} \tag{1}$$

where $M_{\text{act}}$ is memory for storing activations, $M_\theta$ for model parameters $\theta$, $M^\theta_{\text{grad}}$ for gradients of $\theta$, $M_{\text{opt}}$ for optimiser state. We focus on $M_{\text{act}}$ as it dominates other terms in common settings [7]. We derive an approximation of $M_{act}$ as:

$$M_{\text{act}} = 2BSV + 2BSD + N\left[\underbrace{16BSD + 2(BS^2H)}_{attn.\ block}\right]. \tag{2}$$

Detailed derivation of all terms is in Supplementary Sec. 1. The tokenizer determines vocabulary size $V$, which affects memory usage in the input and output layers of the LM (via the $2BSV$ term). Importantly, it also determines indirectly the LM's sequence length $S$, which impacts memory across all layers, including quadratic terms. Words not in the tokenizer's vocabulary are split into multiple tokens (Fig. 1a), increasing $S$ for a given input. As a result, general-purpose tokenizers alongside larger $V$, often require $S$ than domain-specific ones, leading to higher overall memory demands.

## 3 Experiments

### 3.1 Experimental Settings

Table 1. Dataset statistics for the datasets used in this study.

| Dataset | No. Reports | Patients | Studies | Findings Len. $\mu$ ($\sigma$) | Conclusions Len. $\mu$ ($\sigma$) | No. Unique Words | Data split Train | Val | Test |
|---|---|---|---|---|---|---|---|---|---|
| MIMIC-CXR [6] | 215,371 | 63,937 | 218,081 | 49 (23) | 25 (24) | 12,570 | 134,805 | 1078 | 1955 |
| CT-RATE [5] | 22,999 | 21,304 | 25,692 | 196 (72) | 34 (29) | 9,783 | 22,587 | 1,526 | 1,564 |
| PET-CT | 45,717 | 27,323 | 45,781 | 147 (69) | 36 (25) | 14,663 | 27,611 | 5860 | 5862 |

**Data:** Experiments were performed using two public datasets, MIMIC-CXR [6] and CT-RATE [5], along with a private dataset of radiology reports of cancer patients with whole body PET-CT. Statistics about the datasets and the train, validation and testing splits are shown in Table 1. In all experiments, from each report we use the *Findings* section, which details observations in the patient's scan, and the *Conclusion* section, which summarises key findings.

**Tokenizer and Model Training:** We evaluate the effect of different tokenizers and their vocabularies on the quality of report summarisation and memory requirements to train a model. We evaluate 3 types of BPE tokenizers, trained independently prior to any LM training. **General:** First, we adopt the GPT-2 tokenizer [11], trained on varied texts by OpenAI, which has a general-purpose vocabulary of size $V \approx$ 50k. **Medical:** We train a tokenizer on varied medical corpus of PubMed abstracts (similarly to [2,4]) yielding $V = 30k$. **Specific:** Finally, we train 3 domain-specific tokenizers (one per dataset) with vocabularies ranging from 9–11k, where $V$ is set dynamically by retaining tokens occurring at least three times.

Each experiment begins by using a trained tokenizer to preprocess the data. An autoregressive LM is subsequently trained to generate the Conclusion from the Findings tokens (Fig. 1). The LM hyper-parameters used are: $N = 8, H = 8, D = 512, D_{ff} = 2048$, where $D_{ff}$ is the dimensionality of feed forward layers. In each experiment, we set maximum sequence length $S$ for the Transformer's input at the 90th (99th for MIMIC) percentile of the report length. Tokenizers that fragment words more frequently require larger $S$. Given a limited memory budget (48 GBs of 1 NVIDIA A6000), as the tokenizer affects how much memory is required per sample, we adjusted the batch sizes in each experiment to maximize memory utilisation. Details on sequence length and batch size used are in Supplementary Table 1. In addition to training the LM **from scratch** on a dataset, we also investigate the effect of tokenization when the LM is **pre-trained** on a biomedical corpus (PubMed abstracts) before it is *fine-tuned* on the target dataset. Such pre-training is commonly used to enhance LM performance when training data for the target task is limited [9].

**Metrics:** We assess overall language quality using common NLP metrics: BLEU (BL-n) [10], METEOR (M) [1] and ROUGE-L (R-L) [8]. To assess clinical efficacy (CE), we extract disease classification labels from the generated and reference conclusions using automated labellers [5,13], and compare them to compute F1 scores. We calculate average F1 over 14 classes in MIMIC-CXR and 18 classes in CT-RATE, using the CheXbert [13] and RadBERT labellers [5] respectively. No text-based disease labeller exists for PET-CT reports, thus this metric is unavailable in this dataset. As a measure of general factual consistency, we calculate RadGraph-XL F1 [3] over all entity and relation types. We also report cosine similarity using a biomedical BERT [2]. All metrics range from 0 to 1 - higher values indicate a closer match to the reference.

## 3.2 Results

**Table 2.** Performance using different vocabularies when LMs are trained from scratch. Best results per dataset in bold.

| Eval. Dataset | Tokenizer | Pretrain | Vocab size | NLP Metrics | | | CE Metrics | | | |
|---|---|---|---|---|---|---|---|---|---|---|
| | | | | BL-1 | M | R-L | F1 macro | F1 micro | RadXL-F1 | Cos. Sim. |
| MIMIC | Specific | ✗ | 9.1k | **0.273** | **0.364** | **0.344** | **0.514** | **0.604** | **0.270** | **0.813** |
| | Medical | ✗ | 30k | 0.262 | 0.353 | 0.325 | 0.480 | 0.594 | 0.243 | 0.809 |
| | General | ✗ | 50k | 0.162 | 0.262 | 0.214 | 0.399 | 0.504 | 0.164 | 0.700 |
| CT-RATE | Specific | ✗ | 9.4k | **0.369** | **0.450** | **0.423** | **0.477** | **0.547** | **0.196** | **0.835** |
| | Medical | ✗ | 30k | 0.344 | 0.423 | 0.400 | 0.458 | 0.544 | 0.175 | 0.819 |
| | General | ✗ | 50k | 0.339 | 0.415 | 0.395 | 0.402 | 0.479 | 0.192 | 0.822 |
| PET-CT | Specific | ✗ | 11.0k | **0.241** | **0.304** | **0.298** | – | – | **0.126** | **0.844** |
| | Medical | ✗ | 30k | 0.234 | 0.294 | 0.283 | – | – | 0.116 | 0.838 |
| | General | ✗ | 50k | 0.176 | 0.241 | 0.234 | – | – | 0.064 | 0.793 |

We evaluate the impact of different tokenizers on report summarisation performance using held-out test sets from MIMIC-CXR, CT-RATE, and PET-CT. Table 2 shows results for LMs trained from scratch on each dataset with different tokenizers, providing several insights. First, both tokenizers trained on medical text (generic *Medical* and domain-*Specific*) consistently outperform general-purpose tokenizers across all metrics when no pre-training is used (Table 2). The domain-*Specific* outperforms the *Medical* trained on PubMed. This is consistent across reports of all imaging types. Results suggest that when training an LM for a specific task from scratch, practitioners should create domain-specific tokenizers instead of adopting general-purpose vocabularies.

When pre-training a LM before fine-tuning it for a task of interest, a natural question arises: what tokenizer should one use? To assess the impact of tokenizer choice in this scenario, we pre-train LMs using each of the 3 tokenizers on PubMed abstracts, followed by fine-tuning and evaluation on the target dataset. Results are shown in Table 3. Pre-training generally improves performance in comparison to training from scratch, with the largest gains observed

**Table 3.** Results for LMs pre-trained on PubMed followed by dataset-specific fine-tuning. Best results per dataset in bold. Relative (%) change from models without pre-training shown in brackets.

| Eval. Dataset | Tokenizer | Pretrain | Vocab size | NLP Metrics (Δ%) | | | CE Metrics (Δ%) | | | |
|---|---|---|---|---|---|---|---|---|---|---|
| | | | | BL-1 | M | R-L | F1 macro | F1 micro | RadXL-F1 | Cos. Sim. |
| MIMIC | Specific | ✓ | 9.1k | **0.285** (+4.4) | **0.380** (+4.4) | **0.359** (+4.4) | **0.521** (+1.4) | **0.622** (+3.0) | **0.283** (+4.8) | **0.817** (+0.5) |
| | Medical | ✓ | 30k | 0.284 (+8.4) | **0.380** (+7.6) | 0.355 (+9.2) | 0.518 (+7.9) | 0.621 (+4.5) | 0.268 (+10.3) | 0.814 (+0.6) |
| | General | ✓ | 50k | 0.167 (+3.1) | 0.261 (-0.4) | 0.220 (+2.8) | 0.417 (+4.5) | 0.527 (+4.6) | 0.169 (+3.0) | 0.721 (+3.0) |
| CT-RATE | Specific | ✓ | 9.4k | **0.403** (+9.2) | **0.492** (+9.3) | **0.468** (+10.6) | 0.564 (+18.2) | 0.616 (+12.6) | 0.229 (+16.8) | **0.844** (+1.1) |
| | Medical | ✓ | 30k | 0.376 (+9.3) | 0.467 (+10.4) | 0.435 (+8.8) | 0.540 (+17.9) | 0.598 (+9.9) | 0.191 (+9.1) | 0.830 (+1.3) |
| | General | ✓ | 50k | **0.403** (+18.9) | **0.492** (+18.6) | 0.451 (+14.2) | **0.568** (+41.3) | **0.620** (+29.4) | **0.243** (+26.6) | 0.840 (+2.2) |
| PET-CT | Specific | ✓ | 11.0k | **0.238** (-1.2) | **0.302** (-0.7) | **0.280** (-6.0) | – | – | **0.127** (+0.8) | **0.842** (-0.2) |
| | Medical | ✓ | 30k | **0.238** (+1.7) | 0.300 (+2.0) | 0.277 (-2.1) | – | – | 0.120 (+3.4) | 0.840 (+0.2) |
| | General | ✓ | 50k | **0.238** (+35.2) | 0.299 (+24.1) | 0.261 (+11.5) | – | – | 0.123 (+92.2) | 0.833 (+5.0) |

for LMs using the *General* or *Medical* tokenizers. In some cases, these models approach the performance of LMs that use the domain-*Specific* tokenizer. We conjecture that this is because more general tokenizers often break domain-specific terms into many subword units, and pre-training helps the LM learn meaningful relationships between these fragments. In contrast, domain-specific tokenizers preserve such terms as whole units, avoiding this issue. LMs using domain-specific tokenizers retain high overall performance across most settings. This suggests that when the target task is known, it is still recommended to design the tokenizer accordingly before pre-training, as it will shape the model's representations throughout.

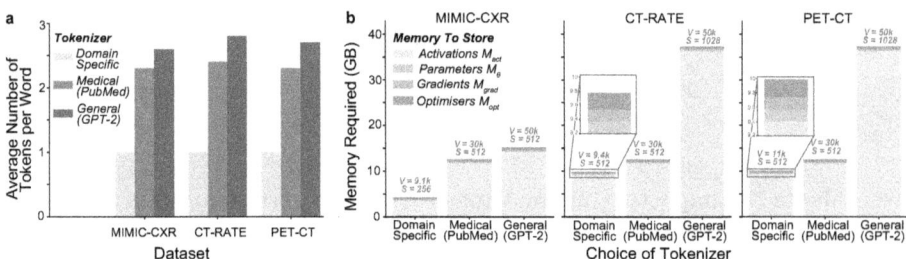

**Fig. 2.** (a) Average number of tokens per word for each dataset and tokenizer. (b) Memory required to train LMs for the different tokenizers, calculated using Eq. 1 for const. batch size B = 32 (max possible for *General* in our GPU). Domain-specific tokenizers produce fewer subword splits, allowing shorter sequences ($S$) which combined with smaller vocabulary size $V$ results in lower memory usage.

Beyond model performance, domain-specific tokenization also reduces the memory required to train the LM. As shown in Fig. 2a and Table 4, the domain-specific tokenizer breaks medical terms into fewer, more meaningful tokens - capturing all words that appear at least 3 times in the dataset, compared to an average of 2.7 tokens per word with the general tokenizer. This more efficient tokenization allows for shorter sequence lengths $S$ which, together with a

**Table 4.** Examples of how 3 tokenizers fragment medical words to tokens.

| Domain specific | Biomedical | General |
|---|---|---|
| bronchovasculature | broncho-vasculature | b-ron-ch-ov-as-cul-ature |
| multinodular | multin-odular | mult-in-od-ular |
| sternomastoid | sterno-mastoid | st-ern-om-ast-oid |

smaller vocabulary $V$, means that domain-specific tokenizers consistently require less memory than a general-purpose tokenizer, as shown in Fig. 2b. We calculate memory requirements using Eq. 1. Domain-specific tokenisation provides efficiency gains which do not compromise the quality of generated reports (Table 2 and 3).

## 4 Conclusion

This study analysed the impact of tokenizers on language modelling for summarising radiology reports of X-rays, CTs and, oncology PET-CTs. Domain-specific tokenizers tailored to each radiology task consistently outperformed general ones, especially when training LMs from scratch. When we pre-train the LMs, the performance gap is reduced, though domain-specific tokenizers still retain consistently high performance across tasks. The study also provided a theoretical analysis of how tokenizers affect memory requirements of LMs, showing that domain-specific tokenizers require substantially less memory than general natural language or medical tokenizers. This can enable LM training with more accessible GPU hardware. These findings highlight the value of task-specific over generic tokenizers when training radiology LMs.

**Acknowledgements.** HW, YI are funded by the EPSRC HDS CDT (EP/S02428X/1). HA is funded by the EPSRC DTP (EP/W524311/1). The work used NHS data from TVS SDE, funded by the UK government and NIHR Oxford Biomedical Research Centre.

## References

1. Banerjee, S., Lavie, A.: METEOR: An automatic metric for MT evaluation with improved correlation with human judgments. ACL Workshop (2005)
2. Boecking, B., et al.: Making the most of text semantics to improve biomedical vision–language processing. ECCV (2022)
3. Delbrouck, J., et al.: RadGraph-XL: A large-scale expert-annotated dataset for entity and relation extraction from radiology reports. ACL (2024)
4. Gu, Y., et al.: Domain-specific language model pretraining for biomedical natural language processing. ACM Transactions on Computing for Healthcare (2022)
5. Hamamci, I.E., et al.: A foundation model utilizing chest CT volumes and radiology reports for supervised-level zero-shot detection of abnormalities. arXiv (2024)

6. Johnson, A., et al.: MIMIC-CXR, a de-identified publicly available database of chest radiographs with free-text reports. Sci. Data (2019)
7. Korthikanti, V., et al.: Reducing activation recomputation in large transformer models (2022)
8. Lin, C.Y., Och, F.J.: Automatic evaluation of machine translation quality using longest common subsequence and skip-bigram statistics. ACL (2004)
9. Liu, C., et al.: A systematic review of deep learning-based research on radiology report generation. arXiv (2023)
10. Papineni, K., et al.: BLEU: a method for automatic evaluation of machine translation. ACL (2002)
11. Radford, A., et al.: Improving language understanding by generative pre-training (2018). OpenAI
12. Sennrich, R., et al.: Neural Machine Translation of Rare Words with Subword Units. ACL (2016)
13. Smit, A., et al.: Combining automatic labelers and expert annotations for accurate radiology report labeling using BERT. EMNLP (2020)
14. Vaswani, A., et al.: Attention is all you need. NeurIPS (2017)

# SCOPE: Speech-Guided COllaborative PErception Framework for Surgical Scene Segmentation

Jecia Z.Y. Mao, Francis X. Creighton, Russell H. Taylor, and Manish Sahu[✉]

Laboratory for Computational Sensing and Robotics, Johns Hopkins University, Baltimore, USA
zmao16@jh.edu, francis.creighton@jhmi.edu, {rht,manish.sahu}@jhu.edu

**Abstract.** Accurate segmentation and tracking of relevant elements of the surgical scene is crucial to enable context-aware intraoperative assistance and decision making. Current solutions remain tethered to domain-specific, supervised models that rely on labeled data and required domain-specific data to adapt to new surgical scenarios and beyond predefined label categories. Recent advances in prompt-driven vision foundation models (VFM) have enabled open-set, zero-shot segmentation across heterogeneous medical images. However, dependence of these models on manual visual or textual cues restricts their deployment in introperative surgical settings. We introduce a speech-guided collaborative perception (SCOPE) framework that integrates reasoning capabilities of large language model (LLM) with perception capabilities of open-set VFMs to support on-the-fly segmentation, labeling and tracking of surgical instruments and anatomy in intraoperative video streams. A key component of this framework is a collaborative perception agent, which generates top candidates of VFM-generated segmentation and incorporates intuitive speech feedback from clinicians to guide the segmentation of surgical instruments in a natural human-machine collaboration paradigm. Afterwards, instruments themselves serve as interactive pointers to label additional elements of the surgical scene. We evaluated our proposed framework on a subset of publicly available Cataract1k dataset and an in-house ex-vivo skull-base dataset to demonstrate its potential to generate on-the-fly segmentation and tracking of surgical scene. Furthermore, we demonstrate its dynamic capabilities through a live mock ex-vivo experiment. This human-AI collaboration paradigm showcase the potential of developing adaptable, hands-free, surgeon-centric tools for dynamic operating-room environments.

**Keywords:** LLM · VFM · STT · TTS · Human-AI collaboration · Computer-assisted intervention

## 1 Introduction

Surgical scene segmentation in endoscopic video is a fundamental task in computer-assisted surgery, enabling downstream tasks such as real-time intraoperative guidance, context-aware assistance, and automated postoperative analysis [7]. Traditional approaches have predominantly relied on deep learning models trained in a supervised fashion on large, manually annotated datasets [1]. While these methods have achieved high accuracy, they struggle to generalize beyond domain-specific data and labels, which restricts their utility in intraoperative settings, where responsiveness to unseen conditions is necessary.

Recent progress in vision foundation models (VFMs) has introduced new possibilities for open-set, prompt-driven segmentation. Models like the Segment Anything Model (SAM) [3] enable category-agnostic segmentation using visual prompts such as clicks or bounding boxes. Grounded SAM (GSAM) [5] extends this paradigm to text-promptable segmentation by integrating open-vocabulary object detection model Grounding DINO [4] to enable text-prompted segmentation across a broad label space. Emerging research in reasoning segmentation models, such as LISA++ [11], explore the use of implicit text queries to support semantically meaningful and context-aware segmentation through multimodal models that combine visual perception with natural language understanding. Together, these advances mark a shift toward more generalizable and interactive systems. However, current interactive methods remain limited by their dependence on manual visual or textual inputs, such as mouse clicks or keyboard-entered queries [6]. While effective for dataset annotation, these interfaces are poorly suited for sterile intraoperative environments. For such systems to be usable in practice, they must fit seamlessly into the surgical workflow and support intuitive, hands-free interaction.

In this work, we introduce a speech-guided collaborative perception (SCOPE) framework tailored for intraoperative use. Our system combines the natural language understanding and reasoning capabilities of large language models (LLMs) with the visual perception of open-set VFMs to enable hands-free, on-the-fly segmentation and tracking of surgical instruments and anatomical structures. At the core of the framework lies a speech-based perception agent that collaborates with the clinician through spoken commands to refine segmentation outputs, label scene elements, and adapt dynamically to evolving surgical contexts.

We evaluate our framework on a publicly available cataract dataset and an in-house ex-vivo microscopic skull-base dataset. Across both datasets, our system demonstrates high performance while offering significant advantages in usability and adaptability. These results highlight the potential of speech-guided, collaborative AI systems for augmenting intraoperative context awareness and decision-making in complex, dynamic surgical environments.

## 2 Related Work

**Promptable Image Segmentation.** Prompt-driven VFMs have significantly advanced generalizable segmentation in medical imaging [12,13]. In the surgical domain, a recent benchmarking study [6] demonstrated superior performance of text-promotable GSAM with Cutie for surgical video annotation task. TPSIS [14] adopted a reasoning segmentation approach [11] approach to addresses class-specific surgical instrument differentiation using transformer-based attention and auxiliary depth cues but remains constrained by its reliance on labeled surgical datasets. Similarly, RSVIS [8] supports referring video segmentation with temporal reasoning across robotic surgery frames, yet it depends on extensive domain adaptation and vocabulary grounding. Rather than fine-tuning on surgery-specific data, which often require massive computational resources and risk overfitting to narrow distributions, we adopted zero-shot VFMs for our framework as we prioritize generalization across procedures and ease of deployment in data-constrained surgical environments.

**Interactive Visual Reasoning.** Frameworks like Visual ChatGPT [9] demonstrate how LLMs can orchestrate vision modules via multimodal prompts, enabling iterative visual reasoning through dialogue. Inspired by this paradigm, our work leverages large language models not merely for communication, but for orchestrating a flexible, speech-driven visual reasoning pipeline. Unlike Visual ChatGPT, which focuses on general visual tasks with static images, our system is designed for dynamic introperative surgical video streams. We emphasize hands-free interaction, real-time adaptability and goal-centric collaboration (Fig. 1).

## 3 Method

### 3.1 System Architecture

Our interactive framework is designed to support natural human-AI collaboration through structured verbal interaction. It uses a cloud-based LLM (GPT-4.1 mini) agent for stepwise reasoning and generate action responses for VFMs to allow users to perform visual tasks through interactive dialogue. The speech AI agent generates responses in the form:

$$\mathcal{R}_i = \{\text{Action}, \text{Text Response}\} = LLM(\mathcal{Q}_i, \mathbb{S}_i, \mathcal{P}, \mathcal{H}_{(<i)})$$

where $\mathcal{Q}_i$ denotes the current user query, $\mathbb{S}_i$ the system inputs, $\mathcal{P}$ the system prompt, and $\mathcal{H}$ the history of prior interactions. The response $\mathcal{R}_i$ guides both the internal function calls to the underlying VFMs and verbal responses to the user. To enable an intuitive and straightforward human-in-the-loop verbal interaction, we created a system prompt $\mathcal{P}$ that defines the system description, constrains and the workflow:

$$\mathcal{P} = \{\mathcal{M}_i, \mathcal{T}_j, \mathcal{E}, \mathcal{R}\}$$

**Module.** $\mathcal{M}$ represent the key phases of interaction to ensure the workflow progresses in a meaningful and context-aware manner. Each module is associated with a specific prompt that defines its entry/exit criteria, allowed tool calls, and in-context examples for user-agent interactions.

$$\mathcal{M} = \{InteractiveMode, Segmentation, SelectMask, Tracking\}$$

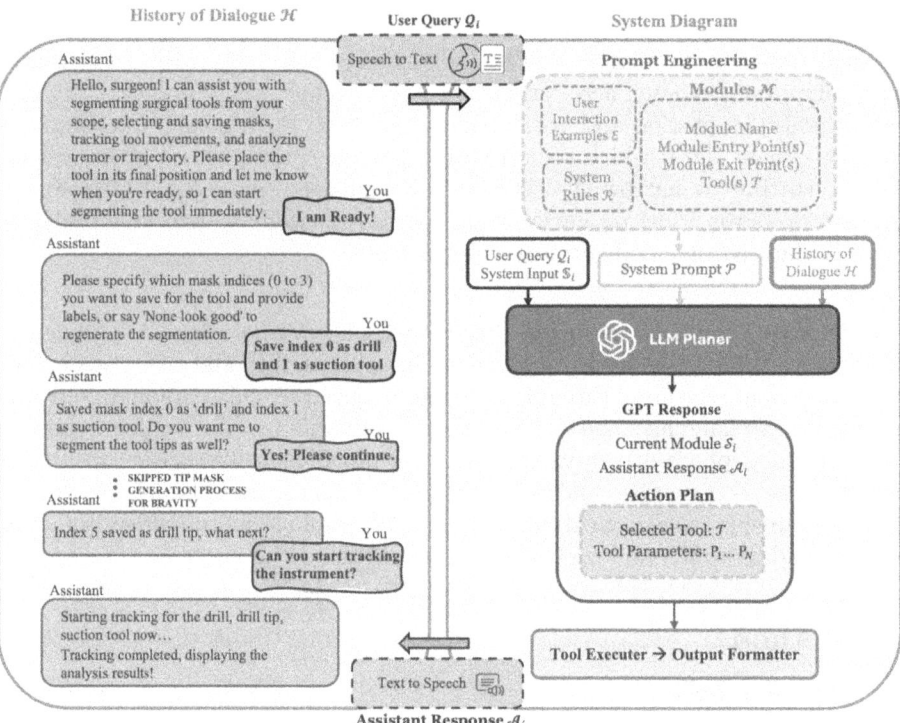

**Fig. 1.** System diagram. Left: tentative user interactions. Right: underlying components that enables such structured workflow.

**Tools.** $\mathcal{T}$ define functional VFM modules invoked at each state. For example, the *segment* tool employs Grounding DINO and SAM to generate segmentation masks from spoken input, while *display* tools assist in visualizing candidates for user selection. Modules guide the sequence of actions, and tools implement the underlying visual computation.

**In-Context Examples.** $\mathcal{E}$ define demonstrations of task-specific queries and expected system behavior to facilitate few-shot generalization by the LLM. These examples guide the agent across states and selecting the appropriate tools.

**Rules.** $\mathcal{R}$ define the structured interactions of the framework. This includes explicit formatting of the output (*JSON* syntax) to enable functional calls.

### 3.2 Interactive Workflow

The system start with the *InteractiveMode* state with a greeting. We use a lavalier microphone, attached to the apron, to stream real-time audio response from the user. The audio input is then transcribed it using OpenAI Whisper. E.g.

given the spoken query (e.g., "segment the surgical instruments" agent transition into the *Segment* state with "surgical instruments" as the text query (Fig. 2).

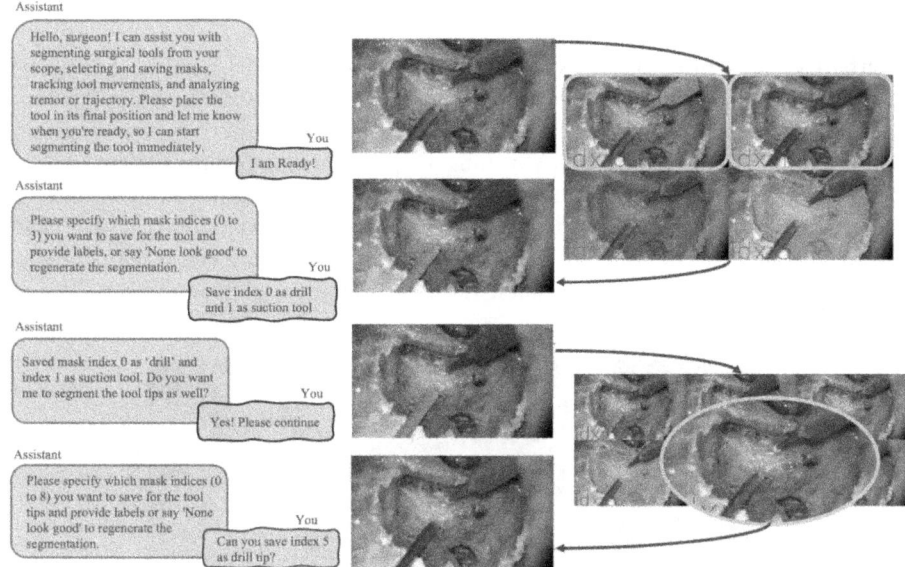

**Fig. 2.** Segmentation workflow: a stage-by-stage visualization of system output while delineating each instrument and its tip.

**Instrument Segmentation and Tracking.** Given a text query (e.g., "surgical instruments"), the query undergoes an expansion process which augments the initial query into semantically similar alternatives (e.g., "surgical tools", "gray instruments") to increase model recall. The spoken command is expanded into semantically related prompts that drive GSAM and LISA++ to generate candidate masks. After applying **ranking heuristics** and deduplication, the six highest-scoring, non-overlapping masks are displayed. This approach eliminates the possibilities of obtaining overly crowded grid for users to select. If none is satisfactory, the system advances to the next **display iteration**. The surgeon verbally selects a mask and assigns its label, completing the segmentation step.

Once instruments are segmented, we use visual promptable VFM for video object segmentation (SAM2 or Cutie) for propagating the mask across video frames. To support tip-based tracking, the system guides the user through another round of segmentation stage to identifying the tip of the instrument. The intersection of the mask boundaries of tip and shaft defines a consistent and geometrically stable tip landmark. For instruments without a distinguishable tip (e.g., suction devices), we instead extract a point along the medial axis of the shaft region, which remains stable due to its rigid geometry. The tip point is tracked by extracting the boundary point along the instrument's principal axis (computed via principal component analysis). We found that this approach generates tracking point that remains consistent across frames without invoking a separate VFM for point tracking.

**Anatomy Segmentation via Virtual Cursor.** We enable hands-free anatomy segmentation with a *virtual cursor* tied to the instrument tip. The cursor's position—offset along the tool's principal axis—is tracked in every frame. A monocular depth VFM (DepthAnything [10]) estimates per-pixel depth; when the tip region contains enough pixels within a preset depth band, a "click" is inferred. The cursor location is then fed to SAM as a positive point prompt, yielding an anatomy mask that is propagated over time by the video-segmentation model, so instruments and contacted tissue are segmented concurrently.

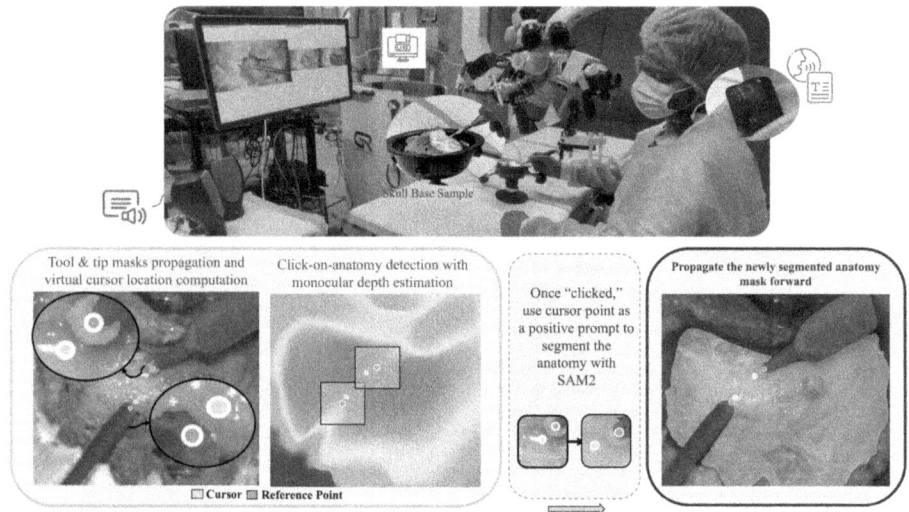

**Fig. 3.** Top: system setup during real-time case study. Bottom: virtual cursor workflow that helps segmenting the anatomy via surface contact.

## 4 Experiments and Results

We benchmarked our two core modules – interactive segmentation and video tracking – on (i) a subset of ten videos of publicly available Cataract1k dataset [2] and (ii) an in-house ex-vivo skull-base dataset containing five videos. Segmentation accuracy is reported with Dice score (DSC) and average surface distance (ASD); tracking quality uses their frame-wise means (mDSC, mASD).

We compared explicit-query GSAM with reasoning-based LISA++ for interactive surgical-tool segmentation. LISA++ prompts were enriched with tool

**Table 1.** Comparison on Initial Segmentation

| Anatomy | Method | DSC | ASD | #Iter. | Time(sec) |
|---|---|---|---|---|---|
| Eye | LISA++ | 0.46 | 26.53 | 1.0 | 4.44 |
|  | GSAM | 0.82 | 2.83 | 1.3 | 1.16 |
| Skull Base | LISA++ | 0.74 | 27.52 | 1.0 | 4.44 |
|  | GSAM | 0.93 | 5.52 | 1.0 | 1.28 |

**Table 2.** Comparison on Mask Propagation

| Anatomy | Method | mDSC | mASD |
|---|---|---|---|
| Eye | CUTIE | 0.840 | 2.736 |
|  | SAM2 | 0.818 | 3.861 |
| Skull Base | CUTIE | 0.973 | 2.54 |
|  | SAM2 | 0.941 | 5.558 |

*Notes.* #Iter.: average number of display iterations until correct mask; Time: runtime per iteration in seconds.

location, appearance, and tissue-interaction cues to encourage instance separation, yet the model still merged multiple instruments in complex cataract scenes. GSAM performed consistently better: with our ranking heuristic it returned the correct mask in the first iteration for 8/10 cataract videos and all 5 skull-base videos, whereas LISA++ was only modestly reliable in simpler one or two-tool skull-base cases (Tables 1 and 2).

For video segmentation and tracking, CUTIE's built-in temporal memory lets it grow the mask as more of the instrument appears, so when a shaft is only partially visible at first and later comes fully into view, the entire tool is automatically captured. In the same scenario SAM2 keeps echoing the original, partial mask, giving CUTIE a clear advantage whenever objects gradually reveal themselves or re-emerge after occlusion.

**Case Study on Live Video Stream.** To assess the usability of our framework in a realistic setting, we conducted a mock surgical experiment (see Fig. 3) on a live surgical video stream. Speech commands, captured by a lavalier mic, prompted Grounded SAM to segment the instruments, while CUTIE handled frame-wise tracking. The correct segmentation mask for surgical instrument is retrieved in the first round; a follow-up isolated its tip, also within the first iteration. Both tool tip and shaft were then stably tracked. When the tip contacted tissue, the system automatically launched anatomy segmentation, confirming seamless end-to-end interactions. For this reason, CUTIE would be more robust in application on surgical scenes.

## 5 Discussion and Conclusion

We present a speech-guided perception system for intraoperative videos that lets surgeons issue natural, hands-free commands to segment and track instruments and anatomy on the fly. Evaluation on two endoscopic datasets and a live mock experiment confirm real-time feasibility. Despite these promising results, the framework has certain limitations. (i) latency of the system response time must be reduced for more efficient interactions; and (ii) our study only a mock procedure, not the full complexity of operating-room workflows. Future work will include evaluating longer, varied cases (laparoscopic, robotic, open), accelerating inference via on-device deployment of originally cloud-based models, and further evaluation to statistically validate the system with surgeon-in-the-loop. These efforts will move the framework from prototype to a deployable assistant that enhances intraoperative context awareness and decision-making.

## 6 Supplementary Material

We aim to release our code and system prompt at https://github.com/LCSR-CIIS/SCOPE.

## References

1. Ahmed, F.A., et al.: Deep learning for surgical instrument recognition and segmentation in robotic-assisted surgeries: a systematic review. Artif. Intell. Rev. **58**(1), 1 (2024)
2. Ghamsarian, N., et al.: Cataract-1k: cataract surgery dataset for scene segmentation, phase recognition, and irregularity detection. arXiv preprint arXiv:2312.06295 (2023)
3. Kirillov, A., et al.: Segment anything. In: ICCV, pp. 4015–4026 (2023)
4. Liu, S., et al.: Grounding dino: marrying dino with grounded pre-training for open-set object detection. In: ECCV, pp. 38–55. Springer (2024)
5. Ren, T., et al.: Grounded sam: assembling open-world models for diverse visual tasks. arXiv preprint arXiv:2401.14159 (2024)
6. Soberanis-Mukul, R.D., et al.: Gsam+ cutie: text-promptable tool mask annotation for endoscopic video. In: CVPR Workshop, pp. 2388–2394 (2024)
7. Vercauteren, T., Unberath, M., Padoy, N., Navab, N.: Cai4cai: the rise of contextual artificial intelligence in computer-assisted interventions. Proc. IEEE **108**(1), 198–214 (2019)
8. Wang, H., et al.: Video-instrument synergistic network for referring video instrument segmentation in robotic surgery. IEEE Trans. Med. Imaging (2024)
9. Wu, C., Yin, S., Qi, W., Wang, X., Tang, Z., Duan, N.: Visual ChatGPT: talking, drawing and editing with visual foundation models. arXiv preprint arXiv:2303.04671 (2023)
10. Yang, L., Kang, B., Huang, Z., Xu, X., Feng, J., Zhao, H.: Depth anything: unleashing the power of large-scale unlabeled data. In: Proceedings of the IEEE/CVF Conference on Computer Vision and Pattern Recognition, pp. 10371–10381 (2024)
11. Yang, S., et al.: Lisa++: an improved baseline for reasoning segmentation with large language model. arXiv preprint arXiv:2312.17240 (2023)
12. Zhang, C., et al.: A survey on segment anything model (sam): vision foundation model meets prompt engineering. arXiv:2306.06211 (2023)
13. Zhou, T., et al.: Image segmentation in foundation model era: a survey. arXiv preprint arXiv:2408.12957 (2024)
14. Zhou, Z., Alabi, O., Wei, M., Vercauteren, T., Shi, M.: Text promptable surgical instrument segmentation with vision-language models. In: NeurIPS, vol. 36 (2023)

# Imagining Alternatives: Towards High-Resolution 3D Counterfactual Medical Image Generation via Language Guidance

Mohamed Mohamed[1,2](✉), Brennan Nichyporuk[1,2], Douglas L. Arnold[1], and Tal Arbel[1,2]

[1] McGill University, Montreal, Canada
[2] Mila – Quebec AI Institute, Montreal, Canada
mohamed.mohamed5@mail.mcgill.ca

**Abstract.** Vision-language models have demonstrated impressive capabilities in generating 2D images under various conditions; however the impressive performance of these models in 2D is largely enabled by extensive, readily available pretrained foundation models. Critically, comparable pretrained foundation models do not exist for 3D, significantly limiting progress in this domain. As a result, the potential of vision-language models to produce high-resolution 3D counterfactual medical images conditioned solely on natural language descriptions remains completely unexplored. Addressing this gap would enable powerful clinical and research applications, such as personalized counterfactual explanations, simulation of disease progression scenarios, and enhanced medical training by visualizing hypothetical medical conditions in realistic detail. Our work takes a meaningful step toward addressing this challenge by introducing a framework capable of generating high-resolution 3D counterfactual medical images of synthesized patients guided by free-form language prompts. We adapt state-of-the-art 3D diffusion models with enhancements from Simple Diffusion and incorporate augmented conditioning to improve text alignment and image quality. To our knowledge, this represents the first demonstration of a language-guided native-3D diffusion model applied specifically to neurological imaging data, where faithful three-dimensional modeling is essential to represent the brain's three-dimensional structure. Through results on two distinct neurological MRI datasets, our framework successfully simulates varying counterfactual lesion loads in Multiple Sclerosis (MS), and cognitive states in Alzheimer's disease, generating high-quality images while preserving subject fidelity in synthetically generated medical images. Our results lay the groundwork for prompt-driven disease progression analysis within 3D medical imaging.

**Keywords:** Vision-Language Models · Counterfactual Image Synthesis · Generative Models · 3D Medical Imaging

## 1 Introduction

Vision-language models have emerged as transformative tools for bridging textual and visual modalities, enabling powerful image synthesis and editing capabilities. Models such as DALL-E [10] and Stable Diffusion [11] exemplify these advancements by producing and modifying high-quality images directly from natural language prompts. The impressive performance of these models in 2D is largely enabled by extensive, readily available pretrained foundation models. Recent innovations, including latent diffusion techniques [11] and instruction-driven image editing methods like InstructPix2Pix [1], have significantly enhanced the ability of these methods to generate photorealistic and semantically precise imagery. Although foundational 2D diffusion models have influenced developments in 3D-aware natural image applications, such as object editing [9], 3D human animation [12], and detailed face generation driven by language attributes [13], existing vision-language methods for 3D predominantly focus on external object surfaces rather than the detailed internal volumetric structures crucial in medical imaging. Critically, comparable pretrained foundation models do not exist for 3D, significantly limiting progress in this domain (Fig. 1).

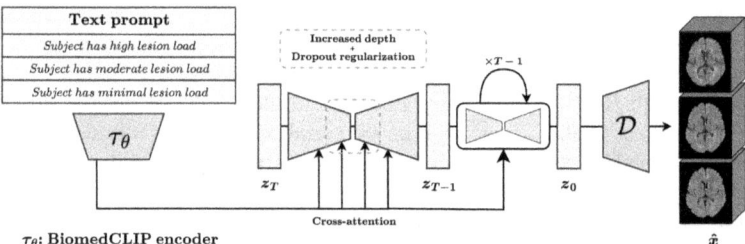

**Fig. 1.** Proposed Framework. A pretrained BiomedCLIP text encoder encodes the text prompt (e.g. "Subject has high lesion load") as conditioning for the diffusion model. During inference, the model generates counterfactuals by sampling from the same fixed noise while varying the text condition.

Medical imaging, particularly neurological imaging, requires accurate volumetric modeling to faithfully represent anatomical complexities inherent in the brain's three-dimensional structure. Recent advances, such as Text2CT [5] and MedSyn [14], have successfully generated anatomically plausible 3D volumes guided by structured medical texts. However, these methods primarily produce novel synthetic scans rather than addressing the clinically important ability to create controlled, counterfactual modifications to existing patient-specific images. Moreover, current methods remain predominantly unconditional or constrained by limited numerical or categorical variables, such as patient age or diagnostic labels [3]. Furthermore, the application of 3D generative models in medical imaging faces substantial challenges, including higher data demands, increased computational complexity, and limited availability of curated volumetric datasets compared to their 2D counterparts.

Addressing this gap, we introduce the first framework capable of generating high-resolution, text-guided 3D counterfactual medical images of *synthetic subjects*, allowing researchers to explore nuanced *what-if* disease-progression scenarios. Unlike prior approaches reliant on slice-based sequential modeling, our approach employs a native-3D, language-guided diffusion backbone, representing the first demonstration of such a model specifically tailored to neurological imaging. We build upon state-of-the-art 3D diffusion architectures, specifically leveraging enhancements from Simple Diffusion [7], such as targeted bottleneck expansion and dropout regularization, alongside incorporating additional cross-attention modules at higher-resolution scales as well as medically-informed semantic embeddings derived from BiomedCLIP [15]. We demonstrate that language-guided wavelet-based diffusion models (WDM), which operate directly in voxel space and support fine-grained counterfactual edits, offer superior subject preservation and achieve text alignment on par with or exceeding that of latent diffusion models. This makes WDM a compelling choice for 3D counterfactual image editing tasks requiring subtle anatomical modifications. In parallel, we enhance the MAISI [4] 3D latent diffusion framework by incorporating a Rectified Flow noise schedule (MAISI RFlow), leading to significant gains in image fidelity and anatomical consistency compared to traditional linear scheduling (MAISI Linear). Notably, MAISI RFlow achieves subject-preservation and text-alignment scores approaching those of WDM, while reducing memory and compute requirements by 65%.

Through extensive experiments on brain MRI datasets representing patients with neurological diseases, our method successfully simulates diverse counterfactual lesion distributions in *synthetic* Multiple Sclerosis (MS) patients and varied cognitive states in *synthetic* Alzheimer's disease patients. Separately, we show how textual alignment and anatomical fidelity can be balanced using classifier-free guidance [6], illustrating the explicit trade-offs inherent to conditional generative modeling. This framework thus lays essential groundwork for leveraging vision-language models in generating counterfactual images of *real* patients, paving the way for personalized disease modeling, realistic clinical image synthesis, and improved medical education in the domain of 3D medical imaging.

## 2 Methodology

In this section we first describe the process of creating text prompts from image-derived features or clinical variables. Next, we describe our language-guided 3D diffusion model architecture and training procedure. Finally, we describe the process of generating language-guided 3D counterfactuals of synthetic patients.

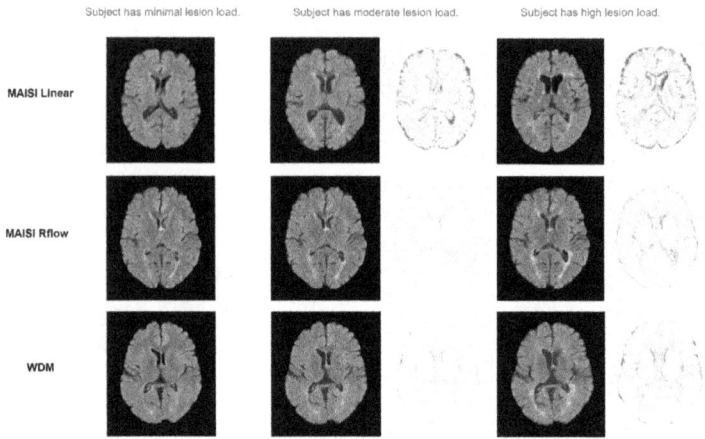

**Fig. 2.** Qualitative comparison of generated counterfactuals for synthesized subjects on the MS dataset for different lesion loads.

### 2.1 Creating Text Prompts

To maximize the effectiveness of text conditioning during inference, we carefully select textual prompts that correspond to prominent and easily distinguishable features in the MRI scans—such as lesion burden or global atrophy patterns. These attributes manifest clearly in the imaging data and help ensure that the model can meaningfully condition on the provided text.

### 2.2 Language-Guided 3D Diffusion Model

We adopt three architectural enhancements inspired by Simple Diffusion [7]. (i) The U-Net bottleneck is deepened with additional residual blocks—an effective way to add capacity with minimal memory/compute overhead. (ii) Targeted dropout is applied in the lower-resolution layers (including the bottleneck) to regularize training and boost image fidelity. (iii) We maximize the use of cross-attention layers at multiple scales, enabling text embeddings to steer both coarse and fine features. During training, we replace the prompt with the null text 20% of the time, enabling classifier-free guidance at inference.

For the noise schedule, we compare the linear schedule of (**WDM**) [3] and the MAISI baseline (**MAISI Linear**) with a rectified-flow variant (**MAISI Rflow**) that follows the straightened diffusion trajectories proposed by Liu et al. [8]. Rectified flow theoretically yields higher sample quality and faster inference by learning an optimal-transport ODE between data and noise.

### 2.3 Generating Language-Guided 3D Counterfactuals

Our counterfactual generation method leverages a text-conditioned diffusion model at inference time to produce samples that differ only in the condition

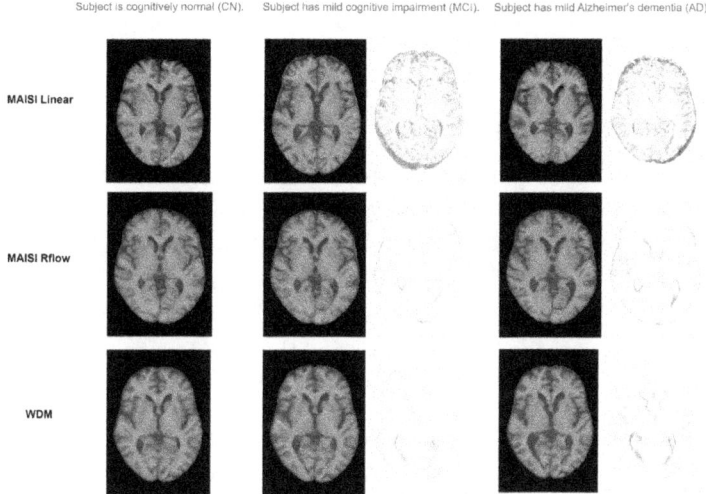

**Fig. 3.** Qualitative comparison of generated counterfactuals for synthesized subjects on the ADNI dataset for different cognitive states.

of interest. During sampling, we start from a fixed source of Gaussian noise and generate images using different text prompts. Formally, let $x_T \sim \mathcal{N}(0, I)$ be a random latent (at the highest diffusion timestep $T$). We generate one image $x_0^{(a)} = D_\theta(x_T, y_a)$ conditioned on text prompt $y_a$ (e.g. "Subject has low lesion load."), and another image $x_0^{(b)} = D_\theta(x_T, y_b)$ from the same noise $x_T$ but with an alternative prompt $y_b$ (e.g. "Subject has high lesion load."). Here $D_\theta(\cdot, y)$ denotes the diffusion model's sampling function decoding noise into an image given condition $y$. This yields counterfactual images that share the same underlying subject identity while reflecting different clinically meaningful states.

## 3 Experiments and Results

### 3.1 Datasets and Implementation Details

We evaluate our approach on two 3D MRI datasets: (1) a proprietary, multi-center dataset of 7107 FLAIR scans from 10 multiple sclerosis (MS) clinical trials, where subjects are grouped by lesion volume into minimal (0–10 mL), moderate (10–25 mL), and high (>25 mL) categories, which are used as text conditions; and (2) the publicly available ADNI dataset comprising 1874 T1-weighted scans labeled as cognitively normal (CN), mild cognitive impairment (MCI), or Alzheimer's disease (AD). Both datasets are split into 70/15/15 for training, validation, and testing. To mitigate class imbalance, we apply weighted sampling to emphasize underrepresented conditions (e.g., high lesion load or AD).

Models are implemented in PyTorch and trained for 1 million steps with a batch size of 1. Latent diffusion models use a DDPM sampler with 1000 denoising steps, while the WDM variant achieved best performance (FID, subject preservation, text alignment) using a DDIM sampler with 25 steps.

## 3.2 Experiments and Metrics

For each model–dataset pair we synthesize 1,000 volumes—333 per prompt—then generate *medium-* and *high-level* counterfactuals from every *low-level* baseline (e.g., low vs. moderate/high lesion burden, cognitively normal vs. MCI/AD). Qualitative examples with difference maps appear in Figs. 2 and 3.

**Table 1.** Performance of the MAISI models and the WDM model for both the MS and ADNI dataset, across image quality, subject preservation, and text alignment accuracy.

| Model | Quality and Diversity | | Subject Preservation | | Text Alignment |
|---|---|---|---|---|---|
| | FID ↓ | MS-SSIM ↓ | MS-SSIM ↑ | PSNR (dB) ↑ | Accuracy (%) ↑ |
| MS Dataset | | | | | |
| MAISI Linear | 0.1734 | **0.8626** | 0.8614 | 21.18 | 92.64 |
| MAISI Rflow | 0.1625 | 0.8715 | 0.9638 | 27.92 | 89.19 |
| WDM | **0.1622** | 0.8684 | **0.9680** | **28.47** | **94.58** |
| ADNI | | | | | |
| MAISI Linear | 0.1752 | 0.8362 | 0.8635 | 22.16 | 62.26 |
| MAISI Rflow | 0.1690 | 0.8357 | 0.9864 | **34.86** | **72.01** |
| WDM | **0.1647** | **0.7485** | **0.9895** | 34.77 | 71.17 |

We evaluate three complementary goals. **(i) Image quality:** realism and diversity are captured by FID (Med3D features [2]; lower is better) and mean MS-SSIM across 1,000 generated samples (lower = more varied). **(ii) Subject preservation:** MS-SSIM and PSNR between each factual image and its counterfactual quantify how faithfully anatomy is retained (higher is better). **(iii) Text alignment:** a 3-D DenseNet-121 classifier is trained to judge whether the generated volume reflects the requested clinical state; its accuracy on held-out *real* scans—96.5% for MS (low vs. high lesion load) and 83.3% for ADNI (CN vs. AD)—provides a strong baseline, so any accuracy drop on counterfactuals reliably indicates misalignment.

## 3.3 Results

In this section, we present qualitative and quantitative results for WDM, MAISI Rflow, and MAISI Linear. Finally, we demonstrate how classifier-free guidance can be used to trade off text-alignment and subject-preservation in the context of counterfactual generation of synthetic subjects.

**Qualitative Counterfactual Generation.** Figures 2 and 3 show counterfactual MRIs generated by our latent diffusion and adapted WDM models. On the MS dataset, MAISI Linear yields low-quality images with off-target changes, whereas MAISI Rflow and WDM selectively increase lesion load while preserving anatomy. The same holds for ADNI: only Rflow and WDM convincingly depict Alzheimer-related cortical atrophy and ventricular enlargement. These results confirm that the rectified-flow noise schedule boosts image fidelity and counterfactual control in latent diffusion models, and that our approach generalizes to voxel-space diffusion via WDM.

**Quantitative Evaluation.** Quantitative results summarizing image quality, subject preservation, and text alignment metrics are reported in Table 1. Language-guided wavelet-based diffusion models (WDM), which operate directly in voxel space and support fine-grained counterfactual edits, offer superior subject preservation on par with or exceeding that of latent diffusion models. They also achieve comparable or superior text alignment, making them an ideal model for subject preserving counterfactual edits. Furthermore, they achieve comparable or superior FID scores on both datasets, indicating superior realism and image quality. In terms of diversity, the WDM baseline yields either the lowest or comparable MS-SSIM scores across generated samples, highlighting superior sample diversity. The MAISI RFlow model achieves subject preservation performance that approaches, or in some cases exceeds that, of the WDM model, but requires 65% less training time, making it a lightweight counterfactual model that can be trained and experimented with quickly in research contexts. Although the MAISI linear model achieved the best sample diversity for the MS dataset, this appeared to stem from, at least in part, exaggerated and unrealistic changes across text prompts, as demonstrated by the worst FID score on the MS dataset. On all other metrics, MAISI linear model almost always achieved the worst performance, making it a poor candidate for fine-grained counterfactual generation in the context of neurological diseases.

**Classifier-Free Guidance Ablation.** Table 2 presents the effects of varying the classifier-free guidance scale ($w$) using MAISI Rflow on the MS dataset. Overall, higher guidance scales significantly enhance prompt fidelity but tend to reduce anatomical consistency. This demonstrates how classifier-free guidance can be tuned to balance text alignment and subject preservation, depending on the researcher's priorities.

Table 2. Ablation of guidance scale (MAISI Rflow on MS).

| Guidance | Text Alignment (%) ↑ | Subject MS-SSIM ↑ | PSNR (dB) ↑ |
|---|---|---|---|
| No CFG | 89.17 | 0.964 | 27.92 |
| 0.5 | 70.08 | 0.985 | 32.30 |
| 1 | 85.96 | 0.964 | 27.89 |
| 2 | 99.39 | 0.926 | 24.39 |
| 3 | 100 | 0.898 | 22.75 |

## 4 Conclusion

In this work, we introduced a novel vision-language framework designed specifically for generating high-resolution, text-guided 3D counterfactual medical images of synthetic neurological subjects. Our approach addresses critical limitations of existing methods by integrating advanced diffusion architectures with medically-informed semantic embeddings derived from BiomedCLIP. The results demonstrate that our language-guided wavelet-based diffusion model (WDM), operating directly in voxel space, delivers superior subject preservation, image quality, and text alignment compared to conventional latent diffusion approaches. Additionally, the MAISI RFlow model, which incorporates a Rectified Flow noise schedule, significantly improves anatomical consistency and image fidelity while achieving computational efficiency. Qualitative and quantitative analyses clearly indicate the effectiveness of these models in simulating nuanced disease-progression scenarios in synthetic Multiple Sclerosis and Alzheimer's patients, and our ablation studies on classifier-free guidance underscore the explicit trade-offs between prompt fidelity and anatomical accuracy. Ultimately, our contributions lay essential groundwork for future extensions towards generating personalized counterfactual medical images from real patient data, with potential implications for enhanced clinical decision-making, personalized disease modeling, and medical education within 3D neurological imaging.

**Acknowledgments.** This investigation was supported by the International Progressive Multiple Sclerosis Alliance (PA-1412-02420) and the companies who generously provided the data: Biogen, BioMS, MedDay, Novartis, Roche/Genentech, and Teva; the MS Society of Canada; the Natural Sciences and Engineering Research Council of Canada; the Canadian Institute for Advanced Research (CIFAR) Artificial Intelligence Chairs program; Calcul Quebec; the Digital Research Alliance of Canada; and Mila - Quebec AI Institute. Data collection and sharing for the Alzheimer's Disease Neuroimaging Initiative (ADNI) dataset is funded by the National Institute on Aging (National Institutes of Health Grant U19AG024904).

**Disclosure of Interests.** The authors have no competing interests to declare.

## References

1. Brooks, T., et al.: InstructPix2Pix: learning to follow image editing instructions. arXiv preprint arXiv:2211.09800 (2023)
2. Chen, S., Ma, K., Zheng, Y.: Med3D: transfer learning for 3D medical image analysis. arXiv preprint arXiv:1904.00625 (2019)
3. Friedrich, P., Wolleb, J., Bieder, F., Durrer, A., Cattin, P.C.: WDM: 3D wavelet diffusion models for high-resolution medical image synthesis. arXiv preprint arXiv:2402.19043 (2024)
4. Guo, P., et al.: MAISI: medical AI for synthetic imaging. In: 2025 IEEE/CVF Winter Conference on Applications of Computer Vision (WACV), pp. 4430–4441 (2025). https://doi.org/10.1109/WACV61041.2025.00435

5. Guo, P., et al.: Text2CT: towards 3D CT volume generation from free-text descriptions using diffusion model. arXiv preprint arXiv:2505.04522 (2025)
6. Ho, J., Salimans, T.: Classifier-free diffusion guidance. arXiv preprint arXiv:2207.12598 (2022)
7. Hoogeboom, E., Heek, J., Salimans, T.: Simple diffusion: end-to-end diffusion for high resolution images. In: Proceedings of the 40th International Conference on Machine Learning (ICML) (2023)
8. Liu, X., Gong, C., Liu, Q.: Flow straight and fast: learning to generate and transfer data with rectified flow. In: Proceedings of the International Conference on Learning Representations (ICLR) (2023)
9. Michel, O., Bhattad, A., et al.: Object 3dit: language-guided 3D-aware image editing. NeurIPS (2023)
10. Ramesh, A., et al.: Zero-shot text-to-image generation. arXiv preprint arXiv:2102.12092 (2021)
11. Rombach, R., Blattmann, A., et al.: High-resolution image synthesis with latent diffusion models. In: CVPR (2022)
12. Wang, Z., Chen, Y., et al.: Humanise: language-conditioned human motion generation in 3D scenes. NeurIPS (2022)
13. Wu, M., Zhu, H., et al.: High-fidelity 3D face generation from natural language descriptions. In: CVPR (2023)
14. Xu, Y., et al.: Medsyn: text-guided anatomy-aware synthesis of high-fidelity 3D CT images. IEEE Trans. Med. Imag. (2024)
15. Zhang, H., et al.: BiomedCLIP: learning biomedical knowledge from million-scale medical image text pairs. Nat. Commun. (2024)

# Pixels Under Pressure: Exploring Fine-Tuning Paradigms for Foundation Models in High-Resolution Medical Imaging

Zahra TehraniNasab[1,2](✉), Amar Kumar[1,2], and Tal Arbel[1,2]

[1] Center for Intelligent Machines, McGill University, Montreal, Canada
[2] Mila – Quebec AI institute, Montreal, Canada
zahra.tehraninasab@mail.mcgill.ca

**Abstract.** Advancements in diffusion-based foundation models have improved text-to-image generation, yet most efforts have been limited to low-resolution settings. As high-resolution image synthesis becomes increasingly essential for various applications, particularly in medical imaging domains, fine-tuning emerges as a crucial mechanism for adapting these powerful pre-trained models to task-specific requirements and data distributions. In this work, we present a systematic study, examining the impact of various fine-tuning techniques on image generation quality when scaling to high resolutions ($512 \times 512$ pixels). We benchmark a diverse set of fine-tuning methods, including full fine-tuning strategies and parameter-efficient fine-tuning (PEFT). We dissect how different fine-tuning methods influence key quality metrics, including Fréchet Inception Distance (FID), Vendi score, and prompt-image alignment. We also evaluate the utility of generated images in a downstream classification task under data-scarce conditions, demonstrating that specific fine-tuning strategies improve both generation fidelity and downstream performance when synthetic images are used for classifier training and evaluation on real images. Our code is accessible through the project website.

**Keywords:** Fine-tuning Foundation Models · Generative Modeling · High-Resolution Image Generation · Text-to-Image Foundation Models

## 1 Introduction

Text-to-Image Foundation models have demonstrated remarkable success across various computer vision tasks, consistently achieving strong performance on standard benchmarks [4, 12][1]. Trained on massive corpora of natural images, these models acquire visual representations, such as textures, shapes, and complex spatial patterns, that often transfer effectively to medical imaging

---
[1] https://tehraninasab.github.io/PixelUPressure/.

domains. This transferability is particularly valuable in clinical settings, where the availability of labeled or paired text-image medical data is scarce. Given the challenges of training large-scale models from scratch with small, specialized datasets, fine-tuning has emerged as a practical and effective strategy for adapting foundation models to medical applications [14,18,23]. Fine-tuning leverages the rich visual priors learned during pretraining, enabling models to be adapted to domain-specific tasks through targeted updates, rather than full retraining [1,25]. In this work, we focus on Stable Diffusion [17] v1.5, a prominent latent diffusion model pre-trained on large-scale natural image-text pairs. While its latent-space architecture enables more efficient high-resolution synthesis compared to pixel-space alternatives, fine-tuning Stable Diffusion on high-resolution medical images still poses significant computational challenges. Scaling to high resolution rapidly increases memory and compute costs, especially for attention-based architectures, posing significant barriers to deployment [25]. These challenges introduce a trade-off between model capacity and computational feasibility, often leading to compromises in generative quality or diagnostic reliability. Addressing this tension is essential for enabling the practical and scalable use of text-to-image foundation models in real-world medical imaging workflows [5].

Recent developments in parameter-efficient fine-tuning (PEFT) methods such as Low-Rank Adaptation (LoRA) [8], DoRA (Decoupled Rank Adaptation) [15], BitFit [24] and Diffusion-specific PEFT (DiffFit) [22], offer promising solutions to these computational scaling challenges by selectively updating model components rather than the entire parameter space [5]. Adapter modules [2,13] offer an alternative approach by inserting small, trainable layers between frozen, pre-trained components, enabling domain-specific adaptation without modifying the original model weights. Despite these methodological advances and their demonstrated effectiveness on standard resolution tasks, the performance characteristics and scaling behaviour of these parameter-efficient approaches in high-resolution medical imaging contexts ($512 \times 512$) remain largely unexplored, particularly regarding their ability to preserve critical diagnostic information while maintaining computational efficiency as input dimensions increase substantially. Previous works by Dutt et al. [5] have analyzed the effect of different strategies to fine-tune at $224 \times 224$ resolution but did not focus on the effect of fine-tuning on image generation quality at higher resolution. Recent work by Davila et al. [3] have compared fine-tuning strategies for image classification in medical imaging, but these images are also at a low resolution of $320 \times 320$ pixels.

This paper presents a comprehensive study of fine-tuning paradigms for high-resolution image generation using Stable Diffusion, a pre-trained diffusion-based text-to-image foundation model. The key contributions of our work are as follows:

- A systematic comparison of fine-tuning strategies—including full fine-tuning and parameter-efficient approaches such as LoRA [8], DoRA [15], BitFit [24], and DiffFit [22]—for $512 \times 512$ image synthesis.
- An in-depth analysis of how these fine-tuning strategies affect generation quality, including visual fidelity (measured by Fr'echet Inception Distance, FID [7]), diversity (via Vendi Score [6]), and prompt-image consistency (evaluated using a classifier-based metric).

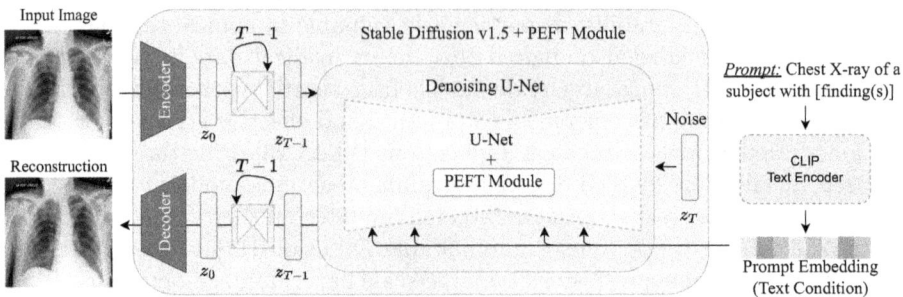

**Fig. 1.** Overview of our architecture. Stable Diffusion v1.5 model is adapted for high-resolution chest X-ray generation using different fine-tuning strategies. The PEFT module shown within the U-Net is only used in parameter-efficient fine-tuning configurations (e.g., LoRA, DoRA, BitFit); in full fine-tuning settings, the U-Net (and optionally the VAE and text encoder) are directly fine-tuned without PEFT modules.

– A downstream evaluation where classifiers are trained on synthetic images and tested on real data, assessing the utility of generated images for real-world diagnostic tasks.

## 2 Methodology

### 2.1 Fine-Tuning Strategies

We evaluate diverse fine-tuning configurations (Fig. 1) for high-resolution image generation through an extensive set of experiments covering combinations of VAE, U-Net, and text encoder using full and parameter-efficient fine-tuning (PEFT); see Table 1. Following [11,21], we generate image-text pairs from tabular data using the template - `Chest X-ray of a subject with [disease(s)]`[2].

**Full Component Fine-Tuning.** For the full component fine-tuning experiments (Models 1–7), we explored the effects of selectively training different combinations of the VAE, Text Encoder, and U-Net modules. This approach allowed us to isolate the contribution of each component to the overall performance of the diffusion model. Some models focused on fine-tuning a single component while freezing the others to assess its standalone impact. For example, Model 1 fine-tuned only the U-Net, while Models 2 and 3 focused solely on the Text Encoder and VAE, respectively. Others involved combinations of two components (Models 4–6) or all three (Model 7).

**Parameter Efficient Fine-Tuning.** To improve efficiency and deployment flexibility, we explored four prominent parameter-efficient fine-tuning strategies:

---

[2] The diseases include: `No Finding, Enlarged Cardiomediastinum, Cardiomegaly, Lung Opacity, Lung Lesion, Edema, Consolidation, Pneumonia, Atelectasis, Pneumothorax, Pleural Effusion, Pleural Other, Fracture,` and `Support Devices`.

**Table 1.** Summary of fine-tuning strategies. ✗: Frozen, ✓: Trainable

| #Model | VAE | Text Encoder | U-Net | Description / Trainable |
|---|---|---|---|---|
| A. Full Fine-Tuning Strategies | | | | |
| 1 | ✗ | ✗ | ✓ | U-Net only |
| 2 | ✗ | ✓ | ✗ | Text Encoder only |
| 3 | ✓ | ✗ | ✗ | VAE only |
| 4 | ✗ | ✓ | ✓ | Text encoder + U-Net |
| 5 | ✓ | ✗ | ✓ | VAE + U-Net |
| 6 | ✓ | ✓ | ✗ | VAE + Text Encoder |
| 7 | ✓ | ✓ | ✓ | U-Net + VAE + Text Encoder |
| B. Parameter-Efficient Fine-Tuning on U-Net | | | | |
| 8 | ✗ | ✗ | ✓ | LoRA [8] |
| 9 | ✗ | ✗ | ✓ | DoRA [15] |
| 10 | ✗ | ✗ | ✓ | BitFit: Only bias terms updated [24] |
| 11 | ✗ | ✗ | ✓ | DiffFit: Diffusion-specific method [22] |

- *Low-Rank Adaptation (LoRA)* [8]: Uses Low-Rank Adaptation to insert trainable low-rank matrices into the network layers, significantly reducing trainable parameters while retaining adaptability.
- *Decoupled Rank Adaptation (DoRA)* [15]: Extends the LoRA framework by decoupling low-rank adaptation into separate direction and scaling components, which allows more flexible control over feature modulation. This approach enhances expressiveness while maintaining parameter efficiency, leading to improved performance under constrained computational budgets.
- *Model 10 (BitFit)* [24]: Restricts training to only the bias terms of each layer, minimizing parameter count to an extreme extent. This model emphasizes the surprising effectiveness of minimal adaptation.
- *Model 11 (DiffFit)* [22]: Employs a diffusion-specific PEFT strategy, leveraging architectural insights tailored to generative diffusion models.

### 2.2 Evaluating Synthesized Images

We evaluate the synthesized medical images for visual quality and their practical utility for downstream clinical applications.

**Image Generation Quality.** Similar to prior work [16,19], we assess image quality using standard metrics covering visual fidelity, and distributional similarity. We employ the Fréchet Inception Distance (FID) [7] to evaluate the distributional similarity between synthesized and real image collections. The Vendi Score [6] measures the diversity of generated samples, complementing FID's realism-oriented evaluation.

Additionally, image-prompt alignment is evaluated at the class level using a pre-trained chest X-ray multi-head Efficient-Net [20] classifier to assess whether the synthesized images accurately reflect their intended diagnostic labels. For each disease condition, a set of 5000 images conditioned on the corresponding textual prompt are generated and passed through the pretrained classifier. Alignment is quantified by measuring the proportion of generated images that are correctly classified into their respective prompted categories, serving as a proxy for semantic faithfulness. This classifier-based evaluation complements distributional metrics by explicitly testing whether disease-specific visual characteristics are preserved and correctly expressed in generated outputs, thus providing a targeted assessment of clinical relevance and prompt adherence.

**Usefulness of the Synthesized Images.** We evaluate the practical utility of these images by training classifiers exclusively on synthetic medical data and testing them on real clinical datasets across multiple disease categories. This provides direct evidence of clinical relevance, measured through standard classification metrics such as accuracy.

## 3 Experiments and Results

### 3.1 Dataset and Implementation Details

We perform experiments on the publicly available CheXpert dataset [10]. All strategies in Table 1 are fine-tuned on the training set mentioned in Table 2. It is important to note that the held-out test set is intentionally made larger than the training set to more rigorously evaluate the generalization performance of the classifier trained on synthesized images. To ensure fair comparison, all methods were fine-tuned on four 80GB H100 GPUs.

**Table 2.** Summary of the train and test splits for the six diseases under observation in CheXpert. Note: Individual images can reflect the presence of several concurrent diseases.

| Class | Training | Validation | Test |
|---|---|---|---|
| Cardiomegaly | 3173 | 1195 | 4515 |
| Lung Opacity | 10269 | 4075 | 14658 |
| Edema | 6447 | 2584 | 9210 |
| No Finding | 1801 | 722 | 2591 |
| Pneumothorax | 2196 | 827 | 3027 |
| Pleural Effusion | 9001 | 3505 | 12972 |

**Metrics Computation.** To compute FID, we use a DenseNet-121 [9] feature extractor pretrained on chest radiographs (via TorchXRayVision), applied to resized $224 \times 224$ grayscale images. For the Vendi Score, 1024-dimensional latent

**Table 3.** Evaluating the quality and consistency of the synthesized images. Ca: Cardiomegaly, Lo: Lung Opacity, Ed: Edema, Nf: No Finding, Pn: Pneumothorax, Pe: Pleural Effusion

| Models<br>Trainable Component | FID↓ | Vendi↑ | Class Consistency↑ | | | | | |
|---|---|---|---|---|---|---|---|---|
| | | | Ca | Lo | Ed | Nf | Pn | Pe |
| U-Net | 3.42 | 5.65 | 24.1 | 10.7 | 25.7 | 91.6 | 15.7 | 21.6 |
| U-Net + Text Encoder | 6.57 | 2.79 | 11.0 | 3.1 | 8.2 | 96.9 | 9.99 | 5.8 |
| U-Net + VAE | 7.46 | 2.59 | 12.1 | 1.0 | 0.7 | 98.1 | 48.0 | 2.0 |
| LoRA [8] | 5.65 | 2.64 | 5.0 | 0.5 | 0.5 | 98.9 | 1.0 | 1.8 |
| DoRA [15] | 5.72 | 3.18 | 8.3 | 0.8 | 0.7 | 98.8 | 0.9 | 1.3 |
| BitFit [24] | 5.05 | 5.89 | 4.8 | 12.6 | 9.8 | 86.4 | 13.4 | 5.0 |

features are extracted from the same DenseNet-121 model. Evaluation is performed on a fixed subset of up to 5,000 real and 5,000 synthetic samples per condition. When fewer than 5,000 real samples are available for a given condition, the number of synthetic samples is matched accordingly. This results in a total of 25,133 real and 25,133 synthetic images used for computing the global FID and Vendi Score, sampled from six target conditions in the held-out test set.

### 3.2 Results

We note that certain fine-tuning configurations, such as those involving only the VAE or only the text encoder, and DiffFit (specifically models # 3, 5, 6, 7 and 11 from Table 1), were excluded from detailed analysis due to consistently poor image quality. These models often produced unrealistic or non-medical outputs, limiting their interpretability and usefulness for downstream evaluation.

**Qualitative Evaluations.** We present a qualitative comparison of generated chest X-ray images across various fine-tuning strategies in Fig. 2. The results highlight the effect full fine-tuning, particularly of the U-Net component in the Stable Diffusion architecture, which serves as the core generative module responsible for denoising and image synthesis. Without updating the U-Net, the model struggles to internalize and reproduce medical features accurately. For this reason, models that omit U-Net fine-tuning, such as those only updating the VAE or Text Encoder, are excluded from Fig. 2, as they tend to produce unrealistic outputs that closely resemble those of the original unadapted Stable Diffusion model. Several parameter-efficient fine-tuning (PEFT) methods yield visually competitive results. Both LoRA and DoRA can reproduce key pathological markers with high visual fidelity, despite training only a small subset of the model parameters. This demonstrates their effectiveness in adapting large generative models to the medical domain with reduced computational cost. In contrast, BitFit, while extremely lightweight, often produces blurrier and less

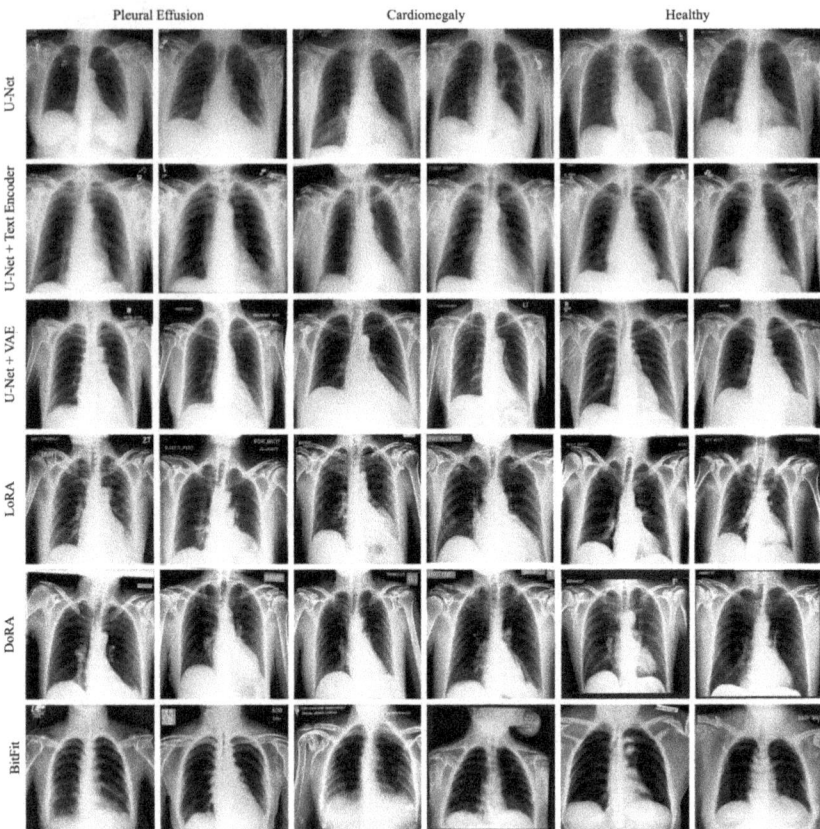

**Fig. 2.** Qualitative comparison of generated chest X-rays across different fine-tuning strategies and three disease categories (Pleural Effusion, Cardiomegaly and Healthy). Each row shows a different fine-tuning method (two samples per disease category). The comparison highlights differences in anatomical plausibility, disease-specific features, and generative fidelity across strategies. Note: Configurations such as those involving only VAE or only text encoder and DiffFit fine-tuning are excluded due to poor image quality.

structurally coherent outputs, particularly in areas where fine-grained anatomical detail is critical. Moreover, in some cases, BitFit produces RGB-like images instead of grayscale radiographs, indicating poor adaptation and suggesting that this method may be insufficient for domain-specific fine-tuning in high-stakes settings such as medical imaging. These qualitative findings suggest that while full-component fine-tuning yields the highest visual fidelity, PEFT strategies provide a compelling trade-off between efficiency and image quality, especially for scalable or resource-constrained deployments.

**Quantitative Evaluations.** Table 3, shows trade-offs between fidelity, diversity, and downstream utility across different fine-tuning strategies. Full fine-

**Table 4.** Accuracy of different model configurations across disease categories. Note: All models are trained and validated on synthetic data and tested on real images.

| Model | Ca | Lo | Ed | Nf | Pn | Pe |
|---|---|---|---|---|---|---|
| U-Net | 37.4 | 48.8 | 67.8 | 90.9 | 89.4 | 51.5 |
| U-Net + Text Encoder | 77.9 | 54.0 | 67.8 | 81.0 | 89.4 | 55.3 |
| U-Net + Vae | 15.7 | 48.8 | 67.5 | 90.9 | 89.4 | 54.7 |
| LoRA [8] | 35.3 | 47.6 | 60.2 | 75.8 | 86.4 | 53.6 |
| DoRA [15] | 80.6 | 47.4 | 52.9 | 75.8 | 89.3 | 52.7 |
| BitFit [24] | 77.3 | 50.9 | 67.8 | 90.9 | 76.4 | 54.5 |

tuning of the U-Net achieves the best FID of 3.42 and strong class consistency scores, particularly for *No Finding* (91.6) and *Lung Opacity* (25.7), confirming the importance of updating the core generative module. Among PEFT methods, LoRA and DoRA achieve competitive FID scores (5.65 and 5.18, respectively) and maintain high class consistency in major categories like *No Finding* and *Pneumothorax*.

When evaluated on real test images after training on synthetic data (Table 4), models fine-tuned on both U-Net and Text Encoder achieve the highest accuracy across nearly all disease categories (e.g., 77.9% for *Cardiomegaly*, 94.8% for *No Finding*), highlighting strong generalization. BitFit also performs surprisingly well in this evaluation, suggesting that while it may underperform in generation quality, its generated images still retain enough semantic structure to be informative for downstream classification. LoRA and DoRA also demonstrate robust cross-domain transfer, particularly in high-signal classes such as *Pneumothorax* and *No Finding*, underscoring their utility as efficient yet effective fine-tuning alternatives.

The PEFT methods show computational advantages, with LoRA requiring only 1.59 million trainable parameters compared to the full U-Net training approaches that utilize between 83.7 million and 98.3 million parameters. Despite this, training times remain comparable, with PEFT methods taking 61–70 s per epoch versus 77–177 s for full training.

## 4 Conclusion

In this work, we systematically evaluated fine-tuning strategies for adapting Stable Diffusion, a text-to-image foundation model, to high-resolution medical imaging tasks. We compared parameter-efficient methods (LoRA, DoRA, BitFit, and DiffFit) against full U-Net training using a comprehensive evaluation framework that assessed both image quality metrics and downstream task performance. Our results demonstrate that full U-Net training outperforms all parameter-efficient methods across evaluation metrics, establishing it as the optimal approach for high-resolution medical image synthesis when computational resources permit.

While parameter-efficient methods successfully address data scarcity challenges in medical imaging domains, the substantial performance gap observed indicates that practitioners should prioritize full U-Net training to achieve maximum diagnostic accuracy. The evaluation methodology developed provides a robust framework for future research by ensuring technical improvements translate to clinical utility. These findings offer clear guidance for deploying foundation models in medical imaging environments and establish performance benchmarks for future parameter-efficient approaches. The work enables informed decisions regarding computational trade-offs in resource-constrained settings while demonstrating the continued superiority of comprehensive network optimization for critical medical applications.

**Acknowledgments.** Funding was provided in part by the Natural Sciences and Engineering Research Council of Canada, the Canadian Institute for Advanced Research (CIFAR) Artificial Intelligence Chairs program, Mila - Quebec AI Institute, Google Research, Calcul Quebec, and the Digital Research Alliance of Canada.

**Disclosure of Interests.** The authors have no competing interests to declare that are relevant to the content of this article.

# References

1. Azad, B., et al.: Foundational models in medical imaging: a comprehensive survey and future vision. arXiv preprint arXiv:2310.18689 (2023)
2. Chen, S., et al.: AdaptFormer: adapting vision transformers for scalable visual recognition. Adv. Neural. Inf. Process. Syst. **35**, 16664–16678 (2022)
3. Davila, A., Colan, J., Hasegawa, Y.: Comparison of fine-tuning strategies for transfer learning in medical image classification. Image Vis. Comput. **146**, 105012 (2024)
4. Dong, X., et al.: InternLM-XComposer2: mastering free-form text-image composition and comprehension in vision-language large model. arXiv preprint arXiv:2401.16420 (2024)
5. Dutt, R., Ericsson, L., Sanchez, P., Tsaftaris, S.A., Hospedales, T.: Parameter-efficient fine-tuning for medical image analysis: the missed opportunity. arXiv preprint arXiv:2305.08252 (2023)
6. Friedman, D., Dieng, A.B.: The vendi score: a diversity evaluation metric for machine learning. arXiv preprint arXiv:2210.02410 (2022)
7. Heusel, M., Ramsauer, H., Unterthiner, T., Nessler, B., Hochreiter, S.: GANs trained by a two time-scale update rule converge to a local Nash equilibrium. Adv. Neural Inf. Process. Syst. **30** (2017)
8. Hu, E.J., et al.: LoRA: low-rank adaptation of large language models. ICLR **1**(2), 3 (2022)
9. Iandola, F., Moskewicz, M., Karayev, S., Girshick, R., Darrell, T., Keutzer, K.: DenseNet: implementing efficient convnet descriptor pyramids. arXiv preprint arXiv:1404.1869 (2014)
10. Irvin, J., et al.: CheXpert: a large chest radiograph dataset with uncertainty labels and expert comparison. In: Proceedings of the AAAI Conference on Artificial Intelligence, vol. 33, pp. 590–597 (2019)

11. Kumar, A., Kriz, A., Havaei, M., Arbel, T.: Prism: high-resolution & precise counterfactual medical image generation using language-guided stable diffusion. MIDL (2025)
12. Li, S., Fu, J., Liu, K., Wang, W., Lin, K.Y., Wu, W.: CosmicMan: a text-to-image foundation model for humans. In: Proceedings of the IEEE/CVF Conference on Computer Vision and Pattern Recognition, pp. 6955–6965 (2024)
13. Li, W.H., Liu, X., Bilen, H.: Cross-domain few-shot learning with task-specific adapters. In: Proceedings of the IEEE/CVF Conference on Computer Vision and Pattern Recognition, pp. 7161–7170 (2022)
14. Liu, G., He, J., Li, P., He, G., Chen, Z., Zhong, S.: PeFoMed: parameter efficient fine-tuning of multimodal large language models for medical imaging. arXiv preprint arXiv:2401.02797 (2024)
15. Liu, S.Y., et al.: DoRA: weight-decomposed low-rank adaptation. In: Forty-First International Conference on Machine Learning (2024)
16. Müller-Franzes, G., et al.: A multimodal comparison of latent denoising diffusion probabilistic models and generative adversarial networks for medical image synthesis. Sci. Rep. **13**(1), 12098 (2023)
17. Rombach, R., Blattmann, A., Lorenz, D., Esser, P., Ommer, B.: High-resolution image synthesis with latent diffusion models. In: Proceedings of the IEEE/CVF Conference on Computer Vision and Pattern Recognition (CVPR), pp. 10684–10695 (2022)
18. Ruffini, F., Ayllon, E.M., Shen, L., Soda, P., Guarrasi, V.: Benchmarking foundation models and parameter-efficient fine-tuning for prognosis prediction in medical imaging. arXiv preprint arXiv:2506.18434 (2025)
19. Saremi, P., Kumar, A., Mohammed, M., TehraniNasab, Z., Arbel, T.: RL4Med-DDPO: reinforcement learning for controlled guidance towards diverse medical image generation using vision-language foundation models. arXiv preprint arXiv:2503.15784 (2025)
20. Tan, M., Le, Q.: EfficientNet: rethinking model scaling for convolutional neural networks. In: International Conference on Machine Learning, pp. 6105–6114. PMLR (2019)
21. TehraniNasab, Z., Kumar, A., Arbel, T.: Language-guided trajectory traversal in disentangled stable diffusion latent space for factorized medical image generation. In: Proceedings of the Computer Vision and Pattern Recognition Conference Workshop Proceedings, pp. 4846–4851 (2025)
22. Xie, E., et al.: DiffFit: unlocking transferability of large diffusion models via simple parameter-efficient fine-tuning. In: Proceedings of the IEEE/CVF International Conference on Computer Vision, pp. 4230–4239 (2023)
23. Yu, Y., Ko, M., Shin, S., Kim, K., Lee, K.: Curriculum fine-tuning of vision foundation model for medical image classification under label noise. Adv. Neural. Inf. Process. Syst. **37**, 18205–18224 (2024)
24. Zaken, E.B., Ravfogel, S., Goldberg, Y.: BitFit: simple parameter-efficient fine-tuning for transformer-based masked language-models. arXiv preprint arXiv:2106.10199 (2021)
25. Zhang, S., Metaxas, D.: On the challenges and perspectives of foundation models for medical image analysis. Med. Image Anal. **91**, 102996 (2024)

# DeepGPT-DILI: Integrating Graph Convolutional Networks and Large Language Model Embeddings for Accurate Drug-Induced Liver Injury Prediction

Minh Huu Nhat Le[1,2], Uyen Khoi Minh Huynh[3], Hong Xuan Ong[4], Phat K. Huynh[5], Minh-Toan Dinh[6], Han Hong Huynh[7], Hien Quang Kha[1], Phat Ky Nguyen[1], Xuan-Loc Huynh[8], An Thuy Vo[9], Thanh-Minh Nguyen[10], Thanh-Huy Nguyen[11], Quan Nguyen[12], and Nguyen Quoc Khanh Le[13,14(✉)]

[1] International Master/PhD Program in Medicine, College of Medicine, Taipei Medical University, Taipei, Taiwan
[2] AIBioMed Group, Taipei Medical University, Taipei, Taiwan
[3] Faculty of Biological Sciences, Nong Lam University, Ho Chi Minh City, Vietnam
[4] Department of Data and Analytics, EPAM, Ho Chi Minh, Vietnam
[5] Department of Industrial and Systems Engineering, North Carolina A&T State University, Greensboro, NC, USA
[6] Department of Software Engineering, University of Science and Technology - The University of Da Nang, Danang, Vietnam
[7] International Master Program for Translational Science, College of Medical Science and Technology, Taipei Medical University, Taipei, Taiwan
[8] Department of Mathematics and Statistics, Boston University, Massachusetts, USA
[9] Can Tho University of Medicine and Pharmacy, Can Tho, Vietnam
[10] School of Medicine, University of Medicine and Pharmacy at Ho Chi Minh City, Ho Chi Minh City, Vietnam
[11] UFR Sciences et Techniques, Université de Bourgogne, Dijon, France
[12] Department of Artificial Intelligence, Posts and Telecommunications Institute of Technology, Ho Chi Minh City, Vietnam
[13] In-Service Master Program in AI in Medicine, College of Medicine, Taipei Medical University, Taipei, Taiwan
khanhlee@tmu.edu.tw
[14] Translational Imaging Research Center, Taipei Medical University Hospital, Taipei, Taiwan

**Abstract.** Drug-induced liver injury (DILI) is a leading cause of late-stage clinical attrition due to its unpredictable onset and potential for severe hepatotoxicity. Therefore, it is necessary to predict hepatotoxic liabilities early and cheaply. The standard approach for this problem is adopting machine learning algorithms traditionally or novel deep learning methods like recurrent neural networks and large language model embeddings. However, there is still a lack of comprehensive assessments of how well these approaches combine. In this study, we benchmark four machine learning models on the 1278-compound DILIRank dataset: (i) extreme gradient boosting (XGBoost); (ii) an ExtraTrees classifier trained on molecular fingerprints reduced via principal component analysis (PCA); (iii) a graph convolutional network (GCN) that encodes atom "bond topology; and (iv) an attention-based recurrent neural network (ARNN) applied to SMILES strings. Large language model (LLM) embeddings enrich both the tabular and graph inputs. The best single learner" ExtraTrees + PCA—achieves an AUC of 0.917. A weight-optimized soft-voting ensemble that fuses fingerprint, graph, LLM, and ARNN outputs further improves performance to an AUC of 0.921 while balancing sensitivity (0.72) and specificity (0.92). These results demonstrate that integrating orthogonal molecular representations yields more reliable hepatotoxicity predictions and offers a practical route for early DILI screening in drug-development pipelines.

**Keywords:** Drug-induced liver injury (DILI) · graph convolutional networks · large language models · ensemble learning · multimodal fusion

# 1 Introduction

Drug-induced liver injury (DILI) is a leading cause of acute liver failure and a major driver of drug termination and withdrawal after market approval. [2,21,23]. Beyond its clinical impact—mortality can reach 10–50% in severe cases—DILI generates multi-million-dollar setbacks across the pharmaceutical pipeline [2,21]. Mechanistically, DILI spans direct hepatocellular toxicity, metabolic activation to reactive intermediates, mitochondrial dysfunction, bile-salt export pump inhibition, and idiosyncratic immune responses, making comprehensive in-vitro screening both labor-intensive and only partially predictive [23]. These limitations have intensified interest in *in-silico* methods that can flag hepatotoxic liabilities early and cheaply.

Early computational efforts relied on quantitative structure–activity relationship (QSAR) models and hand-crafted molecular fingerprints, achieving modest accuracy but suffering from limited chemical coverage and feature bias [7,13]. Recent surveys show that classical machine learning (ML) algorithms, such as random forests, XGBoost, and ExtraTrees, remain competitive when fingerprints are distilled through dimensionality-reduction techniques like principal component analysis (PCA) [6,13]. Deep learning has expanded the molecular toolkit. Graph neural networks (GNNs) [24] treat molecules as atom-bond graphs, capturing both local chemistry and global topology; GNN variants [9,22] (e.g., graph convolutional networks (GNNs), attention-based networks, and geometric-message passers) report the area under the ROC curve (AUC) values above 0.9 on public DILI benchmarks. Parallel advances in chemical language models apply transformer-based or recurrent neural network (RNN) architectures to SMILES strings, producing embeddings that encode higher-order sub-structure and functional-group context [3,14,18]. Large language model (LLM) embeddings have even matched or surpassed domain-specific pre-training in property-prediction and drug-drug-interaction tasks [18].

Although each representation captures different biochemical facets, single-modality models seldom generalize across diverse scaffolds. Ensemble and multimodal fusion strategies (combining fingerprints, graphs, and language embeddings) have proven effective in related toxicity domains, boosting accuracy and robustness over any standalone learner [6]. However, systematic evaluations of such hybrid frameworks for DILI remain sparse. To address that gap, we benchmark systematically to validate the performance of different model combinations for ensembling.

In this paper, our contributions are three-fold. Firstly, we conduct experiments with four complementary learners to verify the performance of each model: (i) extreme gradient boosting (XGBoost); (ii) an ExtraTrees classifier trained on molecular fingerprints reduced via principal component analysis (PCA); (iii) a GCN that encodes atom–bond topology; and (iv) an attention-based RNN (ARNN) applied to SMILES strings. These models are trained on the 1278-compound DILIRank dataset. Next, we improve the performance further to achieve state-of-the-art by fusing their outputs through a weight-optimized soft-voting ensemble. To demonstrate the effectiveness of our method, we compare it with the methods in other related works. Finally, we investigate the contribution of each model to general performance through an ablation study. Besides, we also experiment to assess the impact of fingerprint compression to find the balanced point while applying this technique.

## 2 Materials and Methods

### 2.1 Overall Framework

This work presents a hybrid learning framework that unifies complementary molecular representations to improve the DILI prediction. As illustrated in Fig. 1, canonical SMILES strings are first converted into twelve PaDEL fingerprint families, yielding a 16093-dimensional binary vector that captures substructural and physicochemical motifs [28]. To mitigate redundancy, the fingerprint space is optionally compressed to the top 100 principal components obtained by PCA [17]. In parallel, each molecule is represented as an undirected atom-bond graph and processed by a GCN that encodes local and global topology [24].

LLM embeddings are extracted at the preprocessing stage before any machine learning model training begins. Specifically, SMILES strings are sent to OpenAI's text-embedding-3-large model via API calls to generate 3072-dimensional semantic vectors. These embeddings are then reduced to 10 principal components using PCA and stored as numerical features for downstream machine learning models.

An ARNN directly ingests tokenized SMILES to capture sequential dependencies [16, 25].

The four ML models—XGBoost, PCA-compressed ExtraTrees, GCN, and ARNN—are trained independently with stratified five-fold cross-validation. Their validation AUCs determine non-negative weights that minimize the squared error between the ensemble logit and the ground truth, subject to a

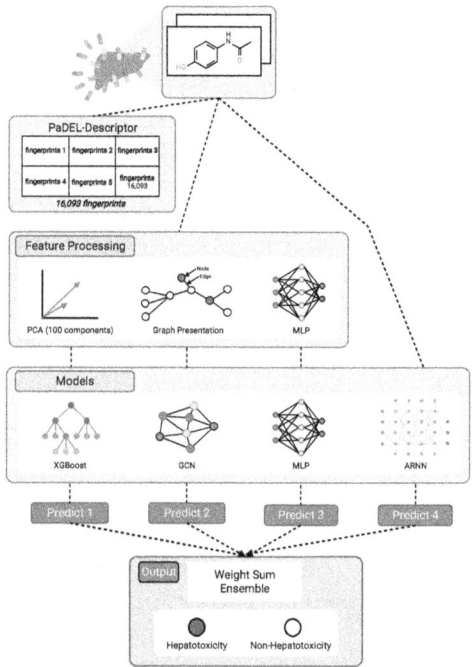

**Fig. 1.** Block diagram of the proposed multimodal ensemble pipeline for DILI prediction. Canonical SMILES are encoded as (i) PaDEL fingerprints, (ii) atom-bond graphs, and (iii) LLM embeddings. After optional feature processing, four specialized learners generate logits that are fused by a weight-summed ensemble to yield a binary hepatotoxicity label. Created in BioRender. Le, M. (2025) https://BioRender.com/wp87smg

unit-sum constraint. The final score is therefore a weighted linear combination of the individual logits, and a threshold of 0.5 discriminates hepatotoxic and non-hepatotoxic compounds [1,12].

### 2.2 Dataset

We use the public *DILIst* corpus [4] from the FDA's Liver Toxicity Knowledge Base, containing 1279 approved drugs labeled as DILI–positive (768) or DILI–negative (511) based on clinical reports. Canonical SMILES were standardized with RDKit 2023.03 [20]: salts and mixtures removed, explicit hydrogens deleted, and stereoisomer duplicates merged. Molecules with missing or conflicting data were excluded.

### 2.3 Representations and Models

Each compound is encoded using three complementary representations: (i) 16,093-bit PaDEL fingerprints (12 families), optionally reduced via PCA to

100 components capturing 95% variance [26]; (ii) atom–bond graphs with 40-dimensional node and 12-dimensional edge features for GCNs [24]; and (iii) 3072-dimensional SMILES embeddings from OpenAI's `text-embedding-3-large` [16]. Additionally, tokenized SMILES are passed through a GRU with Bahdanau attention, using a 38-token vocabulary from [19].

Each representation is paired with a dedicated model: XGBoost uses full fingerprints; ExtraTrees uses PCA-reduced ones. a 5-layer GCN processes molecular graphs; and the attention-based RNN consumes SMILES sequences. Neural models are trained with Adam and dropout; tree models rely on out-of-bag validation and class-balanced weights.

### 2.4 Training and Evaluation Protocol

All models were trained in a stratified 5-fold cross-validation loop maintaining class balance. Within each outer fold, 80% of the data was used for training and 20% for validation during hyperparameter tuning. Neural networks used He initialization, Adam optimizer, exponential learning-rate decay (5% per epoch), and early stopping (patience = 50). Tree ensembles used out-of-bag estimates and class-balanced weights. Ensemble weights were derived from inner validation scores and fixed before outer fold testing to avoid data leakage. Full hyperparameter settings are available at: https://doi.org/10.6084/m9.figshare.29877521.

Model performance was evaluated using five metrics: accuracy (ACC), sensitivity (SE), specificity (SP), precision (PRE), and AUC. Definitions follow standard form, e.g., $SE = TP/(TP + FN)$, $SP = TN/(TN + FP)$, $AUC = \int TPR(f)\, df$. AUC, which summarizes classification over all thresholds and resists class imbalance, is the primary metric. We report mean ± SD over test folds in Sect. 3.

## 3 Experimental Results

### 3.1 Comparison to Existing Work

We benchmarked our model against prior DILI prediction studies from 2010–2023 (Table 1). Early models using Bayesian classifiers and simple SVM/KNN ensembles [5,11] achieved AUCs below 0.70 due to limited fingerprints and small datasets. Later, Zhang et al. [27] improved to 0.75 using MACCS fingerprints but with poor specificity (0.24).

A major performance leap came with multi-fingerprint ensembles. Ai et al. [1] reached AUC 0.904 using 12 fingerprint families; Minerali et al. [12] validated this on DILIrank. More recently, GNNs and DNNs using transcriptomics and molecular graphs approached 0.92 AUC [24].

Our model surpasses all prior work by fusing four complementary views, compressed fingerprints, graphs, LLM embeddings, and SMILES sequences, into a weight-optimized ensemble. It achieves an AUC of 0.921 with a balanced SE = 0.715 and SP = 0.923, highlighting the advantage of combining handcrafted and learned representations.

**Table 1.** Performance comparison of hepatotoxicity prediction models

| Study | Methodology | AUC | SE | SP | Key Features |
|---|---|---|---|---|---|
| Ekins (2010) [5] | Bayesian modeling | 0.620 | 0.528 | 0.655 | Early ligand-based model with limited feature diversity |
| Liew (2011) [11] | Ensemble SVM and k-NN | 0.676 | 0.641 | 0.633 | Mixed learning algorithms and diverse compound dataset |
| Zhang (2016) [27] | SVM with MACCS fingerprints | 0.748 | 0.929 | 0.240 | Focused on substructure pattern recognition using a dataset of 1317 compounds; external validation AUC of 0.75 |
| Ai (2018) [1] | Ensemble learning | 0.904 | 0.869 | 0.754 | 12 molecular fingerprints; external validation with 286 compounds |
| Minerali (2020) [12] | Bayesian, SVM, k-NN | 0.814 | 0.741 | 0.755 | DILIRank data; model comparison using external validations |
| Li (2020) [10] | DNN on transcriptomic profiles | 0.798 | 0.839 | 0.603 | LINCS L1000 dataset; largest binary DILI classification dataset; independent validation |
| Nguyen (2020) [15] | CNN with molecular fingerprints | 0.890 | 0.760 | 0.820 | Integrated molecular fingerprint embeddings into convolutional layers for hepatotoxicity prediction |
| Kang (2021) [8] | DNN (ECFP4 fingerprints) | 0.870 | 0.714 | 0.750 | Used substructure-specific endurance levels; validated on multiple external datasets |
| Yan (2022) [25] | Genetic Algorithm, Ensemble Learning | 0.842 | N/A | N/A | Rotation-Ensemble-GA framework using multi-fingerprint molecular representation; validated via external datasets |
| Wu (2023) [24] | GNN w/ molecular geometric representation | 0.910 | N/A | N/A | Used graph-based geometric representations for robust and interpretable DILI predictions |
| **Our study (2025)** | **GCN, ARNN, Ensemble** | **0.921** | **0.715** | **0.923** | **Integration of graph-based features, OpenAI embeddings, and ensemble strategies** |

## 3.2 Internal Benchmarking and Ablation Study

To quantify the individual and collective contributions of the constituent learners, we conducted a stratified five-fold cross-validation on the curated DILIst set and recorded the mean test-fold metrics; the outcomes are listed in Table 2.

**Ablation Study.** Among single models, **XGB-FP-PCA** achieved the highest AUC (0.9168) with strong precision (0.951), outperforming the full-bit variant **XGB-Base** (AUC = 0.9142). Deep learners like **GCN** and **ARNN** improved recall and precision, respectively, but had lower AUCs ($\leq 0.82$). LLM-only models underperformed (AUC < 0.70).

Combining two streams offered modest gains: **FP-G-Ens** reached 0.9146 AUC, and **FP-OpenAI-Ens** improved precision to 0.9580. Adding a third stream increased robustness: **FP-G-OpenAI-Ens** reached 0.9203 AUC, while **FP-G-AttRNN** slightly boosted recall.

The full four-stream ensemble (**FP-G-OpenAI-AttRNN**) achieved the best overall trade-off: AUC = 0.9208, precision = 0.969, recall = 0.715, and specificity = 0.923. Ablation showed that removing any stream degraded performance—most notably fingerprints (-0.031 AUC).

**Modal Contribution.** Fingerprint models contributed most to AUC. Graph features improved recall by capturing connectivity motifs. OpenAI embeddings

**Table 2.** Performance Comparison of Hepatotoxicity Prediction Models

| Model | Features | AUC | Precision | Recall | Specificity |
|---|---|---|---|---|---|
| XGB-Base | 16093 FP | 0.9142 | 0.9629 | 0.7058 | 0.9076 |
| XGB-FP-PCA | FP (PCA 100) | 0.9168 | 0.9509 | 0.7013 | 0.8769 |
| GCN | Node/Edge | 0.8203 | 0.9000 | 0.6700 | 0.7700 |
| distilbert-base | 768 emb. | 0.6568 | 0.8404 | 0.7149 | 0.5385 |
| bert-base-smiles | 512 emb. | 0.6721 | 0.8333 | 0.7014 | 0.5231 |
| ModernBERT-base | 768 emb. | 0.6876 | 0.8486 | 0.7104 | 0.5692 |
| MLP-LLM | 3072 emb. | 0.6661 | 0.8376 | 0.7239 | 0.5230 |
| MLP-OpenAI-PCA | PCA 10 | 0.6898 | 0.8224 | 0.7964 | 0.4154 |
| AttRNN | Attn RNN | 0.7512 | 0.8600 | 0.6900 | 0.6700 |
| FP-G-Ens | 2 scores | 0.9146 | 0.9461 | 0.7149 | 0.8615 |
| FP-OpenAI-Ens | 2 scores | 0.9163 | 0.9580 | 0.7239 | 0.8923 |
| FP-G-OpenAI-Ens | 3 scores | 0.9203 | 0.9636 | 0.7194 | 0.9076 |
| FP-G-AttRNN | 3 scores | 0.9165 | 0.9580 | 0.7239 | 0.8923 |
| **FP-G-OpenAI-ARNN** | **4 scores** | **0.9208** | **0.9693** | **0.7149** | **0.9230** |

enhanced precision via semantic cues. The ARNN helped refine decisions on rare or long SMILES sequences.

### 3.3 Effect of Fingerprint Compression

To assess dimensionality reduction, XGBoost was retrained using different numbers of PCA components from the 16,093-bit fingerprint vector. AUC rose sharply from 0.861 (raw) to 0.903 with just 10 components and peaked at 0.915 with 100. Beyond 200 components, performance declined. Using 100 components preserved 95% variance, reduced training time by 60%, and offered the best bias–variance trade-off.

## 4 Discussion and Conclusion

We present a multimodal DILI prediction pipeline that fuses molecular fingerprints, graphs, LLM embeddings, and SMILES encodings. Ablation confirms that each stream contributes distinct signals. Our final ensemble achieves SOTA AUC (0.921), balancing SE (0.715) and SP (0.923).

While LLM embeddings alone achieved modest performance (AUC < 0.70), they play a pivotal role in the ensemble framework. The OpenAI embeddings contribute 8.7% weight in the final ensemble and enhance precision by capturing semantic relationships between molecular structures that conventional fingerprints may miss. Unlike fingerprints that encode explicit substructures, LLM embeddings provide implicit representations learned from vast chemical language patterns, offering complementary information that improves overall prediction robustness. The weight optimization demonstrates that LLM embeddings provide unique signals that cannot be replicated by other modalities.

Compared to past QSAR or single-view deep models, our method improves generalization and robustness. Limitations include lack of external validation and ensemble interpretability. Future work will focus on metabolite-aware modeling, speed–accuracy trade-offs, and deployment in active-learning frameworks for continual refinement.

**Acknowledgement.** This work is supported by the National Science and Technology Council, Taiwan [grant numbers MOST111-2628-E-038-002-MY3 and NSTC114-2221-E-038-015.

# References

1. Ai, H., Chen, W., Zhang, L.: Predicting drug-induced liver injury using ensemble learning methods and molecular fingerprints. Toxicol. Sci. **165**(1), 100–107 (2018). https://doi.org/10.1093/toxsci/kfy121
2. Babai, S., Auclert, L., Le-Louët, H.: Safety data and withdrawal of hepatotoxic drugs. Therapies **76**(6), 715–723 (2021)
3. Barranco-Altirriba, M., Würf, V., Manzini, E., Pauling, J.K., Perera-Lluna, A.: Smile-to-BERT: a BERT architecture trained for physicochemical properties prediction and smiles embeddings generation. bioRxiv, p. 2024–10 (2024)
4. Chen, M., Suzuki, A., Thakkar, S., Yu, K., Hu, C., Tong, W.: DILIrank: the largest reference drug list ranked by the risk for developing drug-induced liver injury in humans. Drug Discov. Today **21**(4), 648–653 (2016)
5. Ekins, S., Williams, A.J., Xu, J.J.: A predictive ligand-based Bayesian model for human drug-induced liver injury. Drug Metab. Dispos. **38**(12), 2302–2308 (2010). https://doi.org/10.1124/dmd.110.034710
6. Feng, H., et al.: Predicting the reproductive toxicity of chemicals using ensemble learning methods and molecular fingerprints. Toxicol. Lett. **340**, 4–14 (2021)
7. Guo, W., et al.: Review of machine learning and deep learning models for toxicity prediction. Exp. Biol. Med. **248**(21), 1952–1973 (2023)
8. Kang, M.G., Kang, N.S.: Predictive model for drug-induced liver injury using deep neural networks based on substructure space. Molecules **26**(24), 7548 (2021). https://doi.org/10.3390/molecules26247548
9. Lee, T., Posma, J.: Improving drug-induced liver injury prediction using graph neural networks with augmented graph features from molecular optimisation (2025)
10. Li, T., et al.: Deep learning on high-throughput transcriptomics to predict drug-induced liver injury. Front. Bioeng. Biotechnol. **8**, 562677 (2020)
11. Liew, C.Y., Lim, Y.C., Yap, C.W.: Mixed learning algorithms and features ensemble in hepatotoxicity prediction. J. Comput. Aided Mol. Des. **25**(9), 855–871 (2011). https://doi.org/10.1007/s10822-011-9448-1
12. Minerali, E., et al.: Comparing machine learning algorithms for predicting drug-induced liver injury (DILI). Mol. Pharm. **17**(7), 2628–2637 (2020)
13. Mostafa, F., Howle, V., Chen, M.: Machine learning to predict drug-induced liver injury and its validation on failed drug candidates in development. Toxics **12**(6), 385 (2024)

14. Mswahili, M.E., Jeong, Y.S.: Transformer-based models for chemical smiles representation: a comprehensive literature review. Heliyon (2024)
15. Nguyen-Vo, T.H., et al.: Predicting drug-induced liver injury using convolutional neural network and molecular fingerprint-embedded features. ACS Omega **5**(39), 25432–25439 (2020)
16. OpenAI: GPT-4 technical report. arXiv preprint arXiv:2303.08774 (2023)
17. Przybylak, K.R., Cronin, M.T.: In silico models for drug-induced liver injury current status. Expert Opin. Drug Metab. Toxicol. **8**(2), 201–217 (2012). https://doi.org/10.1517/17425255.2012.651419
18. Sadeghi, S., Bui, A., Forooghi, A., Lu, J., Ngom, A.: Can large language models understand molecules? BMC Bioinf. **25**(1), 225 (2024)
19. Seal, S., et al.: Improved detection of drug-induced liver injury by integrating predicted in vivo and in vitro data. Chem. Res. Toxicol. **37**(8), 1290–1305 (2024)
20. Tahıl, G., Delorme, F., Berre, D., Monflier, É., Sayede, A., Tilloy, S.: Stereoisomers are not machine learning's best friends. J. Chem. Inf. Model. **64**(14), 5451–5469 (2024)
21. Tiwari, V., et al.: Insights into medication-induced liver injury: understanding and management strategies. Toxicol. Rep., 101976 (2025)
22. Wang, J., et al.: Predicting drug-induced liver injury using graph attention mechanism and molecular fingerprints. Methods **221**, 18–26 (2024)
23. Weber, S., Gerbes, A.L.: Challenges and future of drug-induced liver injury research laboratory tests. Int. J. Mol. Sci. **23**(11), 6049 (2022)
24. Wu, W., et al.: GeoDILI: a robust and interpretable model for drug-induced liver injury prediction using graph neural network-based molecular geometric representation. Chem. Res. Toxicol. **36**(11), 1717–1730 (2023)
25. Yan, B., et al.: An algorithm framework for drug-induced liver injury prediction based on genetic algorithm and ensemble learning. Molecules **27**(10), 3112 (2022)
26. Yap, C.W.: Padel-descriptor: an open source software to calculate molecular descriptors and fingerprints. J. Comput. Chem. **32**(7), 1466–1474 (2011)
27. Zhang, C., Cheng, F., Li, W.: In silico prediction of drug-induced liver toxicity using substructure pattern recognition method. Mol. Inf. **35**(3), 136–146 (2016). https://doi.org/10.1002/minf.201501020
28. Zhang, L., et al.: Support vector machine models for predicting drug-induced liver injury. Chem. Res. Toxicol. **29**, 623–632 (2016)

# From Reports to Relations: Large Language Models for Knowledge Graph Extraction in Digital Pathology

Karthik Prathaban[1,2](✉)[iD], Farhan Akram[2][iD], Stefan Klein[1][iD], and Martijn P. A. Starmans[1,2][iD]

[1] Department of Radiology and Nuclear Medicine, Erasmus MC Cancer Institute, University Medical Center Rotterdam., Rotterdam, The Netherlands
k.prathaban@erasmusmc.nl
[2] Department of Pathology, Erasmus MC Cancer Institute, University Medical Center Rotterdam., Rotterdam, The Netherlands

**Abstract.** Large language models (LLMs) are increasingly used to structure free-text clinical data. However, many practical approaches rely on rigid schema-based outputs, which limit semantic flexibility and downstream reuse. In this study, we propose an alternative representation: prompting an open-weight LLM to directly extract knowledge graph triples. Unlike findings in pre-defined field-based outputs such as JSON, graph-based outputs naturally capture relationships between entities, supporting more flexible querying, integration, and visualization. We apply our method to a curated subset of Dutch soft tissue tumor pathology reports and compare the graph-based extractions with structured JSON outputs. Across 20 reports for 24 specimens, both formats achieved high macro-averaged F1 scores ($\geq 0.9$) for most fields, with JSON marginally outperforming in certain categories. In addition to their competitive accuracy, graph outputs offer improved structural consistency and semantic clarity, making them a promising foundation for generating ground-truth labels in downstream tasks such as imaging-based AI applications. These findings support the use of knowledge graph-based outputs as a solution for structuring complex medical narratives.

**Keywords:** Large Language Models · Knowledge Graphs · Digital Pathology

## 1 Introduction and Related Work

The digitalization of clinical workflows has resulted in greater accessibility to clinical reports across healthcare institutions. In domains such as pathology, these reports contain rich diagnostic and descriptive information that is essential for both research, including medical image analysis, and clinical decision-making. However, the unstructured free-text nature of these reports poses significant challenges, especially in integration with other modalities.

Large Language models (LLMs) have shown strong potential in structuring clinical text through the extraction of predefined structured data. Their zero and few-shot capabilities have made them attractive candidates for medical information extraction, especially in low-resource scenarios where training data is limited and manually curated annotations are infeasible. While the most common output format is JavaScript Object Notation (JSON) [1–4], prior work has noted that ensuring consistent, parse-able formatting with JSON outputs may require additional engineering efforts or grammar-constrained decoding strategies [1]. Moreover, while JSON is effective for encoding fixed fields, it is not suitable for representing complex or nested biomedical relationships in a semantically expressive and interpretable manner.

Knowledge graphs offer a more flexible alternative to strictly hierarchical formats such as JSON for structuring medical text, and are particularly useful for representing heterogeneous relationships among biomedical entities. In clinical informatics, large-scale knowledge graphs such as Hetionet and PrimeKG have demonstrated broad utility across applications like drug repurposing, phenotype–genotype association, and literature-based discovery [5, 6]. Recent studies have explored LLMs as a tool for knowledge graph construction directly from clinical reports, bypassing the need for extensive manual curation or complex rule-based systems [7, 8]. These examples highlight the potential of LLMs to facilitate the construction of semantically rich biomedical graphs from unstructured pathology narratives. However, to our knowledge, no prior work has systematically evaluated the use of LLMs for extracting knowledge graph specifically from pathology reports.

In this study, we present a proof-of-concept evaluation of using a large language model to extract structured knowledge graph triples from pathology reports. The approach is compared to a more conventional rule-based method that outputs JSON, using a shared subset of clinically relevant features, including diagnosis, mitosis, necrosis, and biomarkers. For each approach, structured information is extracted with the open-weight Phi-4 language model and a few-shot prompt. The dataset comprises 20 Dutch pathology reports containing findings of 24 tissue specimens from patients with soft tissue tumors, providing a challenging and illustrative example due to their rarity.

## 2 Methods

### 2.1 Dataset

We collected Dutch pathology reports of 20 patients with soft-tissue tumor biopsies from 2010 to 2024 from Erasmus University Medical Center, Rotterdam, the Netherlands. Reports were selected from a database of lipomatous tumors based on the presence of a confirmed tumor diagnosis, descriptive information across multiple clinically relevant fields (e.g., mitotic activity, necrosis, molecular markers), and anatomical diversity. This ensured that each report contributed to a diverse and representative set of outputs suitable for evaluating structured extraction performance. In particular, the selected cases span benign and malignant diagnoses (e.g., lipoma, atypical lipomatous tumor (ALT), dedifferentiated liposarcoma), a range of anatomical sites (e.g., retroperitoneum, adrenal gland, femur, axilla), and variable molecular marker expressions (e.g., MDM2 amplification, S100 negativity).

To ensure relevance to downstream clinical and research applications, this study focused on fields commonly used as ground truth annotations for imaging-based AI models in digital pathology:

- Anatomical site: For spatial context and alignment with imaging.
- Tumor diagnosis: To support classification or phenotyping.
- Mitosis and necrosis: Key prognostic indicators often reflected in histology.
- Biomarker or gene expression findings: Targets or correlates in phenotyping or prognosis prediction tasks.

This field selection informed the design of each prompt, ensuring alignment with anticipated downstream use cases in medical AI.

## 2.2 Model Selection and Prompting Strategies

The open-weight Phi-4 language model (14B parameters) was used for all extractions [9]. Phi-4 was selected for its strong performance on reasoning-heavy tasks, having demonstrated the ability to surpass its teacher model, GPT-4, on STEM-focused question answering benchmarks despite its smaller size [9, 10]. Additionally, the model is relatively well-suited for local deployment without requiring heavy resources, running at full precision on dual NVIDIA RTX A6000 GPUs. We designed two prompting templates to guide Phi-4: one for producing structured JSON outputs, and one for generating knowledge graph triples.

**Table 1.** Mapping of shared clinical fields between JSON keys and graph predicates used in prompting. Each row outlines the correspondence between structured output fields used in the JSON format and the equivalent predicate names used in the knowledge graph format.

| Field | JSON key | Graph Predicate |
| --- | --- | --- |
| Anatomical Site | organ_or_site | located_in |
| Tumor Diagnosis | tumor_diagnosis | shows_tumor_diagnosis |
| Mitosis | mitotic_activity | shows_mitotic_activity |
| Necrosis | necrosis_presence | shows_necrosis_presence |
| markers | marker_results | shows_marker_result |

The structured output schemas for both JSON and graph-based prompts were aligned across shared clinical fields, as shown in Table 1. The JSON-based prompt instructs the model to return a list of dictionaries—one per anatomical site—as pathology reports often describe findings from multiple tissue regions. Each dictionary contains the following fields: organ_or_site, tumor_diagnosis, mitotic_activity, necrosis_presence, and marker_results. All values were returned as strings, except for marker_results, which was structured as a dictionary of marker-expression pairs.

The graph-based prompt instructs the model to represent biomedical facts as a list of (subject, predicate, object) triples. Predicates are limited to a fixed schema: shows_tumor_diagnosis, shows_mitotic_activity, shows_necrosis_presence, shows_marker_result, and located_in. The predicates were deliberately phrased to align with natural sentence structure, enabling intuitive interpretation of triples as readable assertions (e.g., "the lesion shows tumor diagnosis myxoid liposarcoma"). Subjects were defined in the prompt as anatomical locations or lesion-specific identifiers (e.g., "inguinal lymph node"), using the site name directly when only one was mentioned, and assigning unique labels when tissue specimens from multiple sites were described.

Both prompts were few-shot in nature, each containing two worked examples to demonstrate the desired output format, with one example demonstrating the expected output for a report describing one tissue section and another example demonstrating the expected output for a report describing multiple tissue sections. They also included explicit instructions to translate Dutch-language reports into English and to avoid inferring or hallucinating information not present in the source text.

Inference was performed using the HuggingFace implementation of the Phi-4 model and wrapped in a LangChain HuggingFacePipeline interface [10, 11, 12]. Prompt texts were dynamically constructed per report by injecting the full pathology report text into a shared prompt template. Lightweight post-processing was used to normalize and validate model outputs. This template defined extraction rules, output formatting, and example demonstrations, ensuring that each model call was tailored to the specific content of the report while maintaining a consistent instruction set. For JSON-format extractions, the model outputs were validated to ensure they were well-formed lists of dictionaries. For graph-based outputs, tuple-based Python lists were parsed, and subject–predicate–object consistency was verified to ensure well-formed triples.

### 2.3 Evaluation Protocol

For each report, true positives (TP), false positives (FP) and false negatives (FN) were manually annotated for five clinical fields: organ_or_site, tumor_diagnosis, mitosis, necrosis, and markers. Per-report precision, recall, and F1 score were computed. If a report had no relevant ground-truth annotations or predicted items for a given field (i.e., $TP = FP = FN = 0$, but TN (True Negative) $> 0$), a perfect score of 1.0 was assigned for that metric to reflect correct absentation by the model. Otherwise, precision, recall, and F1 were computed normally or marked as undefined (NaN) when denominators were zero.

Macro-averaged metrics were reported for each field by averaging the per-report precision, recall, and F1 scores across all reports with at least one relevant annotation or prediction (i.e., $TP + FP + FN > 0$). Reports without any annotations or predictions were excluded from the macro average to prevent inflated performance estimates.

## 3 Results

### 3.1 Quantitative Performance Comparison

Table 2 reports macro-averaged precision, recall and F1 scores across 24 specimens from 20 Dutch pathology reports, comparing structured field extraction using JSON and graph-based output formats. Overall, both formats yielded high performance across most fields, particularly for tumor_diagnosis (JSON: F1 = 0.99; Graph: F1 = 0.98) and markers (JSON: F1 = 0.96; Graph: F1 = 0.91). The JSON format slightly outperformed the graph-based approach in most categories, though the margin was small and context-dependent.

Notably, organ_or_site showed a higher recall for JSON (0.95) than graph (0.90), though both achieved perfect precision. Manual inspection revealed that most organ recall errors stemmed from translation mismatches. For instance, "rechter kuit" ("right calf") was mistranslated as "right thigh" in both formats, while "li bovenbeen" (abbreviated Dutch for "left thigh") was incorrectly predicted as "femur" with the graph-based method.

The largest performance gap appeared in the necrosis category, where the graph-based format underperformed (recall: 0.77) relative to JSON (recall: 0.95). Two of the three false negatives for the graph format occurred when necrosis was mentioned only in the macroscopy section of the report (e.g. "no solid necrotic or hemorrhagic areas suspicious for dedifferentiation"), without being reiterated microscopically. This behavior may not reflect a model error per se, but rather a prompt-driven interpretation: the graph extraction prompt emphasizes specimen-level findings, often implicitly tied to microscopic observations. The model may have interpreted macroscopic-level findings as out-of-scope.

**Table 2.** Macro-level evaluation metrics for structured field extraction across 20 pathology reports. Each row shows precision, recall, and F1-score, computed at the field level for two output formats: JSON and graph triples. The macro-level metrics were only calculated for reports with an annotation or prediction (TP/FP/FN) in each field. The number of valid reports utilized are mentioned in the table.

| Format | Field | Number of Valid Reports (With TP/FP/FN) | Macro Precision | Macro Recall | Macro F1 |
| --- | --- | --- | --- | --- | --- |
| Graph | organ_or_site | 20 | 1.00 | 0.90 | 0.90 |
| | tumor_diagnosis | 20 | 0.98 | 1.00 | 0.98 |
| | mitosis | 11 | 0.86 | 0.95 | 0.85 |
| | necrosis | 11 | 1.00 | 0.77 | 0.79 |
| | markers | 18 | 1.00 | 0.90 | 0.91 |
| JSON | organ_or_site | 20 | 1.00 | 0.95 | 0.95 |
| | tumor_diagnosis | 20 | 0.98 | 1.00 | 0.99 |
| | mitosis | 9 | 0.94 | 0.94 | 0.93 |

*(continued)*

### 3.2 Qualitative Structural and Relational Comparison

Figure 1 illustrates an example of the model output in both graph and JSON formats, extracted from a Dutch pathology report concerning a biopsy near the right kidney. The extracted findings included a well-differentiated liposarcoma with suspected differentiation, incipient necrosis, no significant mitotic activity, and detailed results for over a dozen biomarkers (e.g. "MDM2: gene amplification", "Vimentin: diffusely strongly positive", "S100: negative").

**Table 2.** (*continued*)

| Format | Field | Number of Valid Reports (With TP/FP/FN) | Macro Precision | Macro Recall | Macro F1 |
|---|---|---|---|---|---|
| | necrosis | 11 | 0.95 | 0.95 | 0.94 |
| | markers | 18 | 1.00 | 0.94 | 0.96 |

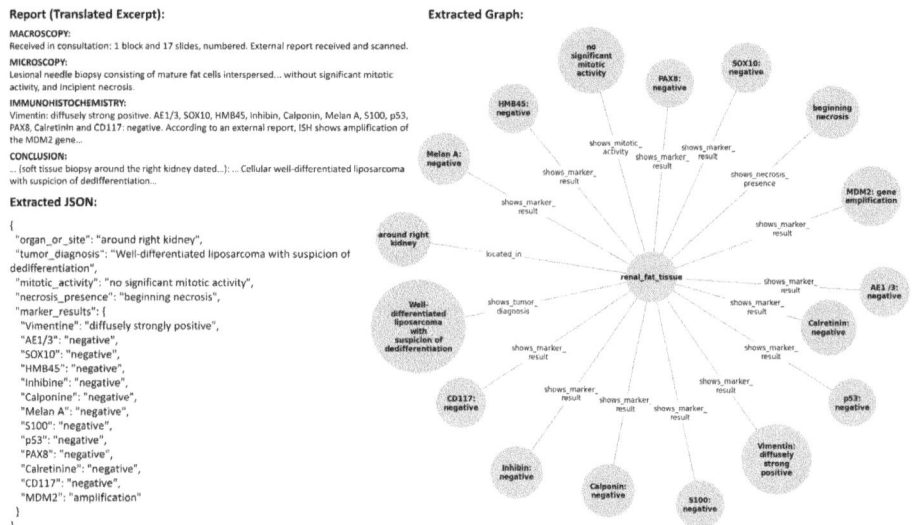

**Fig. 1.** Example of graph-based structured output generated from a Dutch pathology report. The report (top left) is translated to English and summarized to provide only the key information for illustrative purposes. The extracted triples are visualized as a subject–predicate–object knowledge graph (right), where the central subject node corresponds to the specimen (renal fat tissue) and is linked via relation-specific edges to clinical findings. The structured JSON output (bottom left) shows a hierarchical representation, mapping key concepts into nested fields for downstream use.

The JSON format represents this information as a nested dictionary, where all findings are grouped under a single anatomical label ("around right kidney"). In contrast, the graph format encodes each fact as a subject-predicate-object triple, where the central node ("renal_fat_tissue") is linked to clinical attributes through explicit relations (e.g., shows_tumor_diagnosis or shows_marker_result). This structure offers clearer alignment between each finding and its anatomical subject, reducing ambiguity in multi-specimen reports. The visual layout highlights how diverse fields semantically relate to the same tissue sample, while its relational format remains easily extensible to new concepts without modifying the schema. Compared to nested JSON, graphs also integrate more naturally for innovations such as multimodal integration.

## 4 Discussion

This study evaluated two formats for structuring Dutch pathology reports, namely graph-based triples and hierarchical JSON using LLMs. Both formats achieved high macro-level performance across key clinical fields (e.g., tumor diagnosis, mitosis, markers), demonstrating the viability of LLMs for structured data extraction in digital pathology. Despite minor performance differences, both approaches captured most clinically relevant content with high precision and recall.

Our results suggest that graph-based outputs offer unique strengths. Their structured triple format enables easier visualization, consistency across entities, and natural extensibility to additional field types. While JSON slightly outperformed in most categories, the differences were marginal. Notably, the lower recall for necrosis in the graph format stemmed from omissions of macroscopic mentions not reiterated microscopically, suggesting that the model's behavior may reflect strict adherence to the per-specimen focus in the prompt, rather than failure. This highlights how prompt design can shape model outputs and affect downstream usability.

Overall, graph representations are not only competitive in performance but also align well with semantic workflows, offering benefits in interpretability, structural consistency, and potential integration into multimodal AI pipelines. These structured outputs, particularly when tied to specific anatomical sites and tumor findings, can serve as high-quality annotations to support supervised learning tasks in imaging-based AI, such as tumor phenotyping or mutation prediction from histologic images. Because each relationship is formalized as a triple, graph annotations can also be queried flexibly using standard tools (e.g., SPARQL), enabling researchers to filter, group, or analyze findings across large corpora of reports. Future work will explore scaling to more diverse report types, mitigating translation artifacts through domain-adapted fine-tuned models, and evaluating the utility of graph-based pipelines that combine text and image data. A more systematic analysis of translation mismatches, such as mistranslations of anatomical terms or abbreviations, could help guide the use of specialized medical translation models. Additionally, user-centered evaluations could shed light on how such representations support real-world clinical workflows and data curation practices.

**Acknowledgments.** This study was funded the NGF AiNed Fellowship Grants (project number NGF.1607.22.025), which is (partly) financed by the Netherlands Organisation for Scientific Research (NWO).

**Disclosure of Interests.** The authors have no competing interests to declare that are relevant to the content of this article.

## References

1. Wiest, I.C., et al.: Privacy-preserving large language models for structured medical information retrieval. NPJ Digit. Med. **7**, 1–9 (2024). https://doi.org/10.1038/s41746-024-01233-2

2. Wiest, I.C., et al.: LLM-AIX: an open source pipeline for information extraction from unstructured medical text based on privacy preserving large language models. medRxiv. 2024.09.02.24312917 (2024)
3. Adams, L.C., et al.: Leveraging GPT-4 for post hoc transformation of free-text radiology reports into structured reporting: a multilingual feasibility study. Radiology **307**, e230725 (2023). https://doi.org/10.1148/radiol.230725
4. Guluzade, A., et al.: ELMTEX: Fine-tuning large language models for structured clinical information extraction. A Case Study on Clinical Reports (2025). http://arxiv.org/abs/2502.05638
5. Chandak, P., Huang, K., Zitnik, M.: Building a knowledge graph to enable precision medicine. Sci Data. **10**, 67 (2023). https://doi.org/10.1038/s41597-023-01960-3
6. Himmelstein, D.S., et al.: Systematic integration of biomedical knowledge prioritizes drugs for repurposing. eLife. **6**, e26726 (2017). https://doi.org/10.7554/eLife.26726
7. Yang, H., Li, J., Zhang, C., Sierra, A.P., Shen, B.: Large language model-driven knowledge graph construction in sepsis care using multicenter clinical databases: development and usability study. J. Med. Internet Res. **27**, e65537 (2025). https://doi.org/10.2196/65537
8. Khatib, H.S.A., Mittal, S., Rahimi, S., Marhamati, N., Bozorgzad, S.: From patient consultations to graphs: leveraging LLMs for patient journey knowledge graph construction (2025). http://arxiv.org/abs/2503.16533
9. Abdin, M., et al.: Phi-4 technical report (2024). http://arxiv.org/abs/2412.08905
10. OpenAI: GPT-4 technical report (2024). http://arxiv.org/abs/2303.08774
11. Wolf, T., et al.: Transformers: state-of-the-art natural language processing. In: Liu, Q. and Schlangen, D. (eds.) Proceedings of the 2020 Conference on Empirical Methods in Natural Language Processing: System Demonstrations, pp. 38–45. Association for Computational Linguistics, Online (2020). https://doi.org/10.18653/v1/2020.emnlp-demos.6
12. Chase, H.: LangChain (2022). https://github.com/langchain-ai/langchain

# 3D Vision–Language Models with Segmentation-Guided Multimodal Data for Spinal MRI Report Generation

Hoda Helmy[1], Abdullah Hosseini[1], Ahmed Ibrahim[1], Asfand Baig-Mirza[2], Ahmed-Ramadan Sadek[2], and Ahmed Serag[1(✉)]

[1] AI Innovation Lab, Weill Cornell Medicine-Qatar, Doha, Qatar
afs4002@qatar-med.cornell.edu
[2] Barking, Havering and Redbridge University Hospitals Nhs Trust, Romford, UK

**Abstract.** Automated radiology report generation using vision–language models (VLMs) holds significant promise for improving clinical workflow and diagnostic consistency. However, most existing approaches are limited to 2D image inputs and lack explicit incorporation of anatomical priors. In this study, we present a 3D-aware VLM framework designed to generate radiology reports from volumetric spine MRI scans while integrating anatomical segmentation masks to guide clinical relevance. We evaluate four input configurations: a baseline model using unsegmented MRI volumes, and three segmentation-aware variants—V1 (T1-weighted + segmentation), V2 (T2-weighted + segmentation), and V3 (T1- and T2-weighted + segmentation). Quantitative results across five evaluation metrics (BLEU, ROUGE-1, ROUGE-L, METEOR, and BERTScore) show that all segmentation-based variants significantly outperform the baseline, with V3 achieving the highest lexical accuracy and overall report quality. These findings underscore the value of spatial priors and multimodal fusion in improving the generation of structured, clinically meaningful spinal MRI reports.

**Keywords:** Multimodal Language Models · Vision Language Model · Report Generation · Phi3 · Spine Cord MRI

## 1 Introduction

Recent advances in artificial intelligence (AI), particularly vision–language models (VLMs), have transformed the landscape of medical image analysis. VLMs, which combine deep visual understanding with natural language generation, are rapidly emerging as powerful tools for tasks such as automated report generation, image–text retrieval, and visual question answering in medical imaging [1].

The need for such innovation is especially acute in spinal imaging. Magnetic Resonance Imaging (MRI) is the modality of choice for evaluating spinal pathologies due to its superior soft tissue contrast and ability to visualize neural structures [2]. Most AI applications in spinal MRI have focused on tasks such as denoising, artifact reduction, anatomical segmentation, and landmark detection [3], while the automated generation of detailed and clinically meaningful radiology reports remains largely unexplored. This capability is crucial for supporting radiologists and neurosurgeons—by improving diagnostic consistency, enabling faster surgical planning through standardized and comprehensive reporting, and contributing to scalable, high-quality care.

For example, conditions such as Lumbar Spinal Stenosis (LSS)—a degenerative narrowing of the lumbar spinal canal—are prevalent and can progress to severe neurological disorders like Cauda Equina Syndrome (CES) if not detected early [4–7]. Timely and accurate interpretation of spinal MRI is therefore critical for patient outcomes. However, manual analysis remains labor-intensive and highly dependent on expert radiologists—a challenge compounded by workforce shortages and increasing imaging demand [8].

Recently, Yeasin et al. [9] fine-tuned generative image-to-text (GIT) models and demonstrated strong semantic performance on publicly available spinal MRI datasets and associated reports, highlighting the models' ability to generate clinically meaningful narratives. However, a fundamental limitation remains: like most current VLMs in medical imaging, their approach is restricted to 2D image inputs.

In many clinical applications, especially in complex anatomical regions like the spine, critical diagnostic cues are distributed across multiple slices in a 3D volume. Ignoring this spatial continuity can lead to incomplete or inaccurate interpretations, undermining the clinical reliability of automated report generation. Furthermore, existing approaches often overlook the integration of explicit anatomical information, such as segmentation masks, that could guide models toward more precise and contextually relevant findings.

To address these gaps, our work investigates the development of 3D-aware VLMs that leverage full volumetric MRI data and incorporate anatomical segmentation to enhance automated report generation, aiming to improve both diagnostic accuracy and clinical coherence.

## 2 Methodology

### 2.1 Dataset

This study utilizes a publicly available dataset comprising lumbar spine MRI scans and corresponding radiology reports from 515 patients [10]. For each patient, three axial-view RGB images are provided, corresponding to the lower lumbar levels: D3, D4, and D5. Each image includes co-registered T1- and T2-weighted scans acquired for the respective level. Specifically, the red, green, and blue channels of each RGB image represent the registered T1-weighted scan, the registered T2-weighted scan, and the Manhattan distance between the two modalities, respectively. [11].

**Pre-processing.** To move beyond traditional 2D approaches, we treated the three axial slices (D3, D4, D5) as a unified 3D volume for each patient, enabling our model to capture spatial context across contiguous anatomical levels. These 3D image volumes were paired with the corresponding single radiology report per patient, aligning with our goal of generating full-volume reports rather than slice-wise captioning.

To further enhance the model's interpretability and clinical relevance, we incorporated segmentation masks into the 3D input volumes. Each slice contains expert-annotated ground truth masks for four anatomical regions of interest: the Intervertebral Disc (IVD), Posterior Element (PE), Thecal Sac (TS), and the area between Anterior and Posterior vertebral elements (AAP) [11].

In addition to the baseline images provided, we separated the original image channels to generate new composite images, which were subsequently merged into a 3D volume. Specifically, we created the following variations to integrate segmentation data into our vision–language model:

1. **V1:** Each slice is constructed by combining the T1-weighted image (assigned to the red channel) with its corresponding segmentation mask (assigned to the green channel), while the blue channel is filled with zeros.
2. **V2:** Each slice is constructed by combining the T2-weighted image (assigned to the red channel) with its corresponding segmentation mask (assigned to the green channel), while the blue channel is filled with zeros.
3. **V3:** Each slice is constructed using three channels: the T1-weighted image (red channel), the T2-weighted image (green channel), and the corresponding segmentation mask (blue channel).

These three preprocessing strategies were evaluated independently to identify the most effective technique for integrating segmentation information. The objective was to assess how segmentation-aware multimodal inputs influence the quality of generated reports and to evaluate the impact of structural supervision within the VLM architecture.

### 2.2 Vision Language Model and Report Generation

As shown in Fig. 1, our framework introduces a 3D-aware VLM designed to generate radiology reports from volumetric spine MRI scans. The input is a composite 3D MRI volume, which is first processed by a dedicated 3D image encoder. We adopt a 3D Vision Transformer–based encoder that leverages multilayer self-attention to capture spatially aware features within the volumetric data [12]. Following the architecture of the original Vision Transformer (ViT), the encoder partitions the 3D input into non-overlapping patches and applies attention mechanisms across multiple transformer layers to model complex spatial dependencies [13].

The features extracted by the encoder are passed to a 3D Spatial Pooling Perceiver, which compresses the high-dimensional feature map into a compact, semantically meaningful latent space. This is achieved through cross-attention

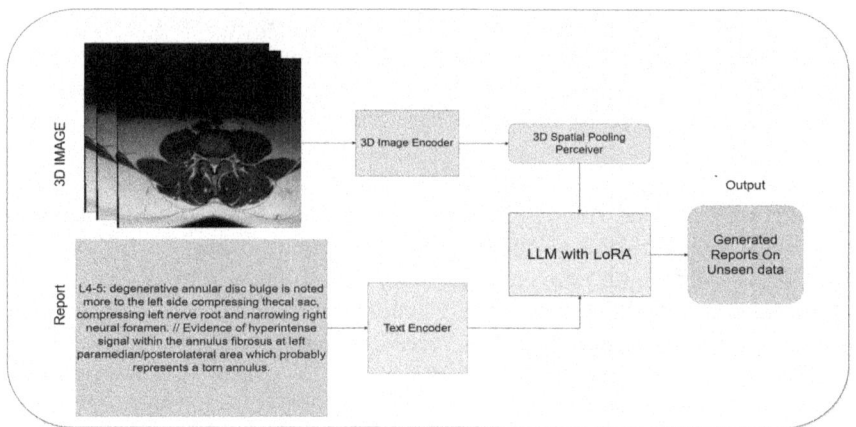

**Fig. 1.** Overview of the proposed 3D vision–language model (VLM) framework for automated spine MRI report generation.

mechanisms, allowing the model to retain both local anatomical details and global contextual information throughout the 3D structure.

In parallel, the corresponding textual radiology report is processed by a Text Encoder, which converts the clinical narrative into a sequence of contextual embeddings. These embeddings capture domain-specific semantics and recurring linguistic patterns commonly found in radiological descriptions.

At the core of our framework is a Large Language Model (LLM), enhanced with Low-Rank Adaptation (LoRA) for efficient fine-tuning. LoRA enables parameter-efficient adaptation by updating only a low-rank subset of the model's weights, significantly reducing computational overhead. The LLM integrates both the visual embeddings derived from the 3D MRI volume and the textual embeddings from the report, learning to align visual features with diagnostic language. During training, the model is supervised to associate spatial representations of the MRI with corresponding clinical descriptions. Once fine-tuned, the system can generate structured, clinically meaningful radiology reports from previously unseen 3D MRI volumes.

### 2.3 Evaluation

Evaluating generated reports in the medical domain requires metrics that comprehensively assess lexical accuracy, coverage, fluency, contextual relevance, and clinical meaningfulness. To this end, we employed a suite of well-established evaluation metrics that, collectively, provide a balanced and robust framework for assessing the quality of automated report generation—capturing both surface-level precision and deeper semantic coherence.

**Precision-Based (Lexical Accuracy) Metrics**

1. **BLEU:** Measures the precision of overlapping n-grams between the generated text and the reference text. It is commonly used to assess lexical accuracy and fluency, though it may penalize valid variations in phrasing.
2. **ROUGE-1:** Calculates unigram (word-level) overlap between the generated and reference texts. It emphasizes keyword-level lexical matching and is often indicative of content relevance.

**Recall-Based (Coverage and Fluency) Metrics**

1. **ROUGE-L:** Measures the longest common subsequence (LCS) between the generated and reference texts. It captures sentence-level fluency, structure, and overall content coverage, emphasizing recall over precision.

**Semantic-Based (Meaning and Contextual Similarity) Metrics**

1. **METEOR:** Evaluates semantic similarity by accounting for exact word matches, synonyms, stemming, and word order. It goes beyond surface-level n-gram overlap, making it well-suited for assessing meaning preservation and paraphrasing quality.
2. **BERTScore:** Leverages contextual embeddings from pretrained language models (e.g., BERT) to compare generated and reference texts at a deeper, context-aware level. It is particularly effective at capturing semantic coherence and nuanced meanings.

We divided the dataset into 70% for training, 20% for validation, and 10% for testing. To account for the limited sample size, to avoid generalization and overfitting, and enhance the reliability of our evaluation, we employed 10-fold cross-validation.

# 3 Results

Figure 2 presents visual comparisons of reports generated by using different input image configurations. In these examples, green text highlights exact word matches with the ground truth, pink text indicates synonyms with equivalent medical meaning, and red text marks incorrect or unrelated terms. While all variarions generated medically relevant content, V3 produced the most accurate report, capturing additional clinically important findings such as Schmorl's nodes and disc desiccation.

In contrast, using 3D images without segmentation (V1) failed to identify the correct diagnosis in this case, incorrectly stating the absence of significant thecal sac or nerve root compression—contradicting the actual findings. Despite minor inaccuracies, the V3 composite clearly produced the most complete and clinically useful report among all input variations.

We conducted experiments using the four distinct imaging variations to quantitatively evaluate the contribution of each MRI modality and the impact

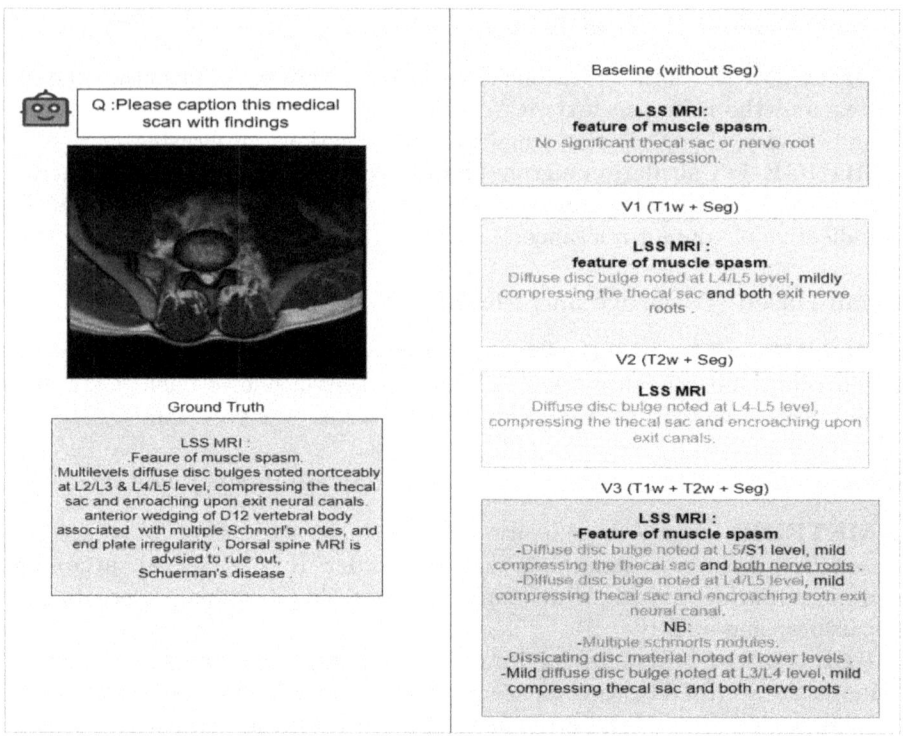

**Fig. 2.** Generated Report output from the VLM models with different stacking techniques. (Color figure online)

of segmentation on spinal MRI report generation. As shown in Table 1, all segmentation-integrated variations (V1, V2, and V3) outperformed the baseline (which lacks segmentation input) across most metrics, confirming the utility of anatomical priors in enhancing report generation.

The baseline model, which relied solely on raw 3D MRI scans without segmentation input, underperformed across all evaluation metrics compared to segmentation-enhanced variants. Its ROUGE-L score (30.08) was notably lower, suggesting difficulty in capturing the structural flow and sentence-level alignment of radiology reports. Similarly, it achieved the lowest BERTScore (88.94), reflecting weaker semantic consistency. These results indicate that models without anatomical guidance from segmentation masks struggle to replicate the detailed and clinically structured language found in expert-written reports.

Both V1 and V2—using images weighed T1 or T2- combined with segmentation, showed strong and consistent performance across all metrics. They tied for the highest BERTScore (89.20), indicating excellent semantic alignment with ground-truth reports. V1 slightly outperformed V2 in BLEU and ROUGE-L, while V2 achieved the highest METEOR score (44.17), which rewards synonymy and paraphrasing. These results suggest that either modality, when paired with

**Table 1.** Comparison of automated spinal MRI report generation across different imaging inputs and model configurations. Evaluation is based on five standard natural language generation metrics: BLEU, ROUGE-1, ROUGE-L, METEOR, and BERTScore. Results are reported for 2D and 3D imaging variations, including baseline and segmentation-aware multimodal settings.

| Experiment | BLUE | ROUGE-1 | ROUGE-L | METEOR | BERTScore |
|---|---|---|---|---|---|
| Baseline (without Seg) | 17.04 | 43.92 | 30.08 | 42.44 | 88.94 |
| V1 (T1w + Seg) | 17.91 | 45.75 | 41.21 | 43.94 | 89.20 |
| V2 (T2w + Seg) | 17.22 | 45.62 | 40.88 | 44.17 | 89.20 |
| V3 (T1w + T2w + Seg) | 18.33 | 44.82 | 40.33 | 43.89 | 89.10 |

segmentation, is effective in generating fluent, accurate, and clinically meaningful narratives.

V3, which integrates both T1- and T2-weighted images along with segmentation masks, achieved the highest BLEU score (18.33), indicating stronger n-gram precision and lexical alignment with the reference reports. Although it slightly underperformed compared to V1 and V2 in some semantic and structural metrics such as ROUGE and METEOR, its consistent and balanced performance across all five evaluation criteria positions it as the most robust model overall. V3 was selected as our model. It leverages the full spectrum of available modalities, including both imaging types and segmentation, leading to more comprehensive and clinically detailed report generation.

## 4 Conclusion

This study investigated the effectiveness of integrating anatomical segmentation and multimodal MRI inputs into 3D VLMs for spinal MRI report generation. Our experiments demonstrated that models leveraging segmentation, particularly V3—which combines T1- and T2-weighted images with segmentation masks—consistently outperformed the baseline in both lexical accuracy and semantic coherence. These results highlight the importance of spatial priors and multimodal fusion in generating clinically meaningful radiology reports. Future work will focus on expanding the evaluation using larger datasets that cover a broader range of spinal pathologies, and extending the framework to support multi-view. This will enable more robust generalization and better alignment with real-world clinical scenarios.

**Acknowledgments.** We acknowledge the support of the IT team at WCM-Q.

**Disclosure of Interests.** The authors declare no conflicts of interest.

## References

1. Li, C., et al.: LLaVA-Med: training a large language-and-vision assistant for biomedicine in one day. arXiv preprint arXiv:2306.00890 (2023)
2. Henninger, B., et al.: Cervical disc and ligamentous injury in hyperextension trauma: MRI and intraoperative correlation. J. Neuroimaging **30**(1), 104–109 (2020)
3. Lee, A., et al.: Applications of artificial intelligence and machine learning in spine MRI. Bioengineering **11**(9), 894 (2024). https://doi.org/10.3390/bioengineering11090894
4. Brøgger, H.A., Maribo, T., Christensen, R., Schiøttz-Christensen, B.: Comparative effectiveness and prognostic factors for outcome of surgical and non-surgical management of lumbar spinal stenosis in an elderly population: protocol for an observational study. BMJ Open **8**(12), e024949 (2018). https://doi.org/10.1136/bmjopen-2018-024949
5. Steurer, J., Roner, S., Gnannt, R., Hodler, J.: LumbSten research collaboration: quantitative radiologic criteria for the diagnosis of lumbar spinal stenosis: a systematic literature review. BMC Musculoskelet. Disord. **12**, 175 (2011). https://doi.org/10.1186/1471-2474-12-175
6. Baig Mirza, A., et al.: The impact of prolapse to canal ratio (PCR) in cauda equina syndrome outcomes and operative management. Eur. Spine J. (2025). https://doi.org/10.1007/s00586-025-08816-x
7. Berg, E.J., Ashurst, J.V.: Anatomy, back, cauda equina. In: StatPearls [Internet]. StatPearls Publishing, Treasure Island (FL) (2023). PMID: 30020623
8. Pal, R., et al.: Lumbar spine tumor segmentation and localization in T2 MRI images using AI. arXiv preprint arXiv:2405.04023 (2024)
9. Yeasin, M., Moinuddin, K.A., Havugimana, F., Wang, L., Park, P.: Auto-rad: end-to-end report generation from lumbar spine MRI using vision-language model. J. Clin. Med. **13**(23), 7092 (2024). https://doi.org/10.3390/jcm13237092
10. Sudirman, S., et al.: Label image ground truth data for lumbar spine MRI dataset. Mendeley Data (2019). https://doi.org/10.17632/zbf6b4pttk.2
11. Al-Kafri, A.S., et al.: Boundary delineation of MRI images for lumbar spinal stenosis detection through semantic segmentation using deep neural networks. IEEE Access **7**, 43487–43501 (2019). https://doi.org/10.1109/ACCESS.2019.2908002
12. Bai, F., Du, Y., Huang, T., Meng, M.Q.-H., Zhao, B.: M3D: advancing 3D medical image analysis with multi-modal large language models. arXiv preprint arXiv:2404.00578 (2024)
13. Dosovitskiy, A., et al.: An image is worth 16 × 16 words: transformers for image recognition at scale. arXiv preprint arXiv:2010.11929 (2021)

# Author Index

**A**
Akram, Farhan  107
Aktar, Mumu  10
Aliakbari Mamaghani, Zeinab  45
Anthony, Harry  62
Arbel, Tal  79, 88
Arnold, Douglas L.  79

**B**
Bagci, Ulas  1
Baig-Mirza, Asfand  115
Belghiti, Khaoula Alaoui  28
Bento, Mariana  10
Binh, Nam Le Nguyen  1
Bosshart, Salome Lou  10

**C**
Chu, Kailin  19
Creighton, Francis X.  71

**D**
Dehaghani, Mehrdad Eshraghi  19
Dinh, Minh-Toan  98

**H**
Helmy, Hoda  115
Heng, Yue  53
Hosseini, Abdullah  115
Huynh, Han Hong  98
Huynh, Phat K.  98
Huynh, Uyen Khoi Minh  98
Huynh, Xuan-Loc  98
Hwang, Soojin  36

**I**
Ibrahim, Ahmed  115
Ibrahim, Yasin  62

**J**
Jindal, Gunjan  10

**K**
Kamnitsas, Konstantinos  62
Katzmann, Alexander  45
Kha, Hien Quang  98
Kim, Won Hwa  36
Klein, Stefan  107
Kumar, Amar  88

**L**
Le, Minh Huu Nhat  98
Le, Nguyen Quoc Khanh  98

**M**
Maier, Andreas  45
Mao, Jecia Z. Y.  71
McGowan, Daniel R.  62
Mikram, Mounia  28
Mohamed, Mohamed  79
Moradi, Mehdi  19
Mori, Kensaku  53

**N**
Nguyen, Khang C.  53
Nguyen, Le Thien Phuc  1
Nguyen, Phat Ky  98
Nguyen, Quan  1, 98
Nguyen, Thanh-Huy  1, 98
Nguyen, Thanh-Minh  98
Nichyporuk, Brennan  79

**O**
Oda, Masahiro  53
Ong, Hong Xuan  98
Ospel, Johanna  10

**P**
Paiva, Pedro  10
Prathaban, Karthik  107

**Q**

Qi, Chuan Y. 53
Quang, Ngoc Bui Lam 1

**R**
Rhanoui, Maryem 28

**S**
Sabour, Amirhossein 19
Sadek, Ahmed-Ramadan 115
Sahu, Manish 71
Serag, Ahmed 115
Shi, Zong X. 53
Sim, Jaeyoon 36
Souza, Roberto 10
Starmans, Martijn P. A. 107
Stebner, Alexander 10

**T**
Taubmann, Oliver 45
Taylor, Russell H. 71
TehraniNasab, Zahra 88

**V**
Vo, An Thuy 98
Vorberg, Linda 45

**W**
Wang, Cheng 53
Warr, Hermione 62

**X**
Xu, Wentian 62

**Z**
Zekaoui, Nour Eddine 28

GPSR Compliance

The European Union's (EU) General Product Safety Regulation (GPSR) is a set of rules that requires consumer products to be safe and our obligations to ensure this.

If you have any concerns about our products, you can contact us on

ProductSafety@springernature.com

In case Publisher is established outside the EU, the EU authorized representative is:

Springer Nature Customer Service Center GmbH
Europaplatz 3
69115 Heidelberg, Germany

www.ingramcontent.com/pod-product-compliance
Lightning Source LLC
Chambersburg PA
CBHW071429261025
34550CB00013B/160